# Genealogy Tip of the Day

*Henry, Bernard, Ehme, Foche, Tjode, Heipke, Anna (nee Dirks), and John Goldenstein. Taken 1892, Basco, Hancock County, Illinois.*

# Genealogy Tip of the Day

December 2008-June 2011

*Michael John Neill*

**ISBN:** 978-0-578-61290-4

*Dedication*

*To my ancestors:*

*who have more stories than I will ever know.*

# Contents

*Charles, Herschel, Nellie, and Fannie (Rampley) Neill, about 1920, St. Albans Township, Hancock County, Illinois*

# Introduction

This is not a typical how-to book.

*Genealogy Tip of the Day* was never meant to provide comprehensive coverage of a topic and each day's tip is meant to be short and readable in no more than a few minutes. It's difficult to do complete justice to most genealogy topics in a short piece of writing. I realize that, but that's not my intent. Our goals with *Genealogy Tip of the Day* are:

- To make the reader aware of something they did not know.
- To remind the reader of something they forgot.
- To help the reader think about the information they find.
- To encourage the reader to think about their research process.
- To occasionally entertain.

This book can be read from front to back, by randomly picking a page, or by browsing the index for a topic. Content reflects my personal research and experiences. Many topics and research concepts apply to most ethnic groups and nationalities and readers are encouraged to think about how an idea may apply to their own personal research. Sometimes I have gotten good conceptual insight into my Virginia ancestors by spending some time working on my Germans. That works in both directions.

Tips that were about "news" items and upcoming events have been removed. That is why there are days with no tip. Items have also been edited for clarity and content and were occasionally expanded from the original posting. Errors in content are my own. The topical index reflects my own use of the tips and includes full names of individuals mentioned but not names mentioned in passing. The index does not include every passing mention of commonly used records. This was to keep the index from becoming an overwhelming part of the book.

Thanks to all who have supported *Genealogy Tip of the Day* in one way or another—especially to all the readers who have been a part of *Tip of the Day* since the beginning. A particular thanks to Jim Beidler, Joe DeRouen, and Michael Leclerc, who provided guidance and suggestions as I began the process of putting some of this material in book form. And again, a great big thanks to all the readers who have been a part of *Genealogy Tip of the Day*. It is appreciated.


—Michael

# Chapter 1: How Grandma Said it, Pond Crossing, Lying, and More

## How Grandma Said It

*14 December 2008*

It took me forever to find Ulfert Behrens in the 1860 and 1870 census. The problem was partially solved when I learned how he likely pronounced his name. This low-German native probably said his last name in a way that sounded something like "barns" to an ear that grew up hearing English. My initial searches focused on names that sounded like "Bear unds" (roughly rhyming with "errands"). Once I started looking for names that sounded like "barns," I found references I had previously overlooked. Recent immigrants are not the only ones whose names can cause these problems. Some members of the long-established American Taliaferro family, long removed from their immigrant ancestor, often pronounce their name in a way that sounds like "toliver." Beauchamp may have been pronounced to sound like "beecham." Find out how your ancestor likely said his name—you may get variant spellings that you never thought to look for.

## Make a Chronology

*15 December 2008*

Looking at things when they are out of order only adds to the chaos. One good organizational technique is to list every event in your ancestor's life from their birth through their death in chronological order. Listing the events in a person's life in the order in which they happened gives the researcher some structure. This also makes it possible to see unaccounted time gaps and possible oversights in your research. A chronology is also an excellent framework from which to write an ancestral biography. This is especially true for those who would like to create a biography of a relative, but don't think they are really "writers" and have no idea where to start. Don't just stop with the events in your relative's life, include the source for every item in your chronology.

## Who Answered Those Census Questions?

*16 December 2008*

For many census records, no matter the time period or location, we do not really know who answered the census questions. Was it the wife who never knew her husband's parents and yet had to answer questions about where they were born? Was it a child who had no idea when her father immigrated to the United States or when he became a citizen? Was it the neighbor who had little clue about the origins of the people who lived next door? Most of us weren't there when the census taker came to our ancestor's door searching for demographic and other information. As a result, we just don't know who really gave the answers to specific questions. If the answers vary from census year to census year, it may be because the individual answering the questions also varied from census year to census year. And it's always worth considering that while you weren't supposed to lie to an enumerator, there is no doubt that it likely happened.

## Those "Wrong" Places May be Clues

*17 December 2008*

In a 1900 census enumeration, several of my great-grandmother's children indicated that their mother was born in Ohio. This seemed completely off the wall to me. All extant records provided Illinois as her place of birth and that place of birth was consistent with when her parents arrived in Illinois. No other record provided Ohio as her birthplace. I almost wrote off "Ohio" as a census taker's goof or some sort of error. While it was wrong, it wasn't quite an error in the way that one may think. Further research revealed the parents of the great-great-grandmother immigrated from Germany, originally settling in Ohio for a few years where they married before moving to Illinois a short time later. By 1900, the great-great-grandmother was dead and her children could easily have thought her parents were "from Ohio" since they had lived and married there. The family did have a connection to Ohio—just not the one that family members thought. Sometimes our ancestors lie, but sometimes incorrect information has significance of which we are simply not yet aware.

## Record Assumptions as Such

*18 December 2008*

We need to make assumptions in our genealogy research. Many times, assumptions are necessary to get our work off the ground and at least make some sort of start. But after a point, it may be that the assumption is hindering our work or that we have even forgotten that an assumption was made. If you are guessing that the parents were married near where the first child was born, that is a reasonable place to start, but somewhere in your notes you might indicate why you believe where they were married and that you have no proof *and that your statement is an assumption*. If research does not validate your assumption, it may be that your assumption was incorrect. And if you enter your assumption in your genealogical database as fact, it can be very difficult for that information to go back to being an assumption—particularly if you published that tree online for others to view. Franciska Beiger was born in Warsaw, Hancock County, Illinois, in 1851, the oldest child of her parents. My initial assumption was that her parents were married in Illinois. That assumption was incorrect. Peter Bieger and Barbara Siefert were married in Cincinnati, Ohio, in 1850, a few months before heading west to Illinois. My assumption was a good place to begin from, but in this case, it was a little far afield from what actually took place.

## Are They Enumerated with Just Initials?

*19 December 2008*

Some census takers were plain lazy, some couldn't spell, and some didn't care. After you have exhausted all the variations on your ancestor's first and middle names while searching for them in an online database, consider that they might have been enumerated with just their initials. Or perhaps they were listed with their first initial and their middle name spelled out. I have seen entire townships where no one apparently had a first name and everyone was listed with only their last name spelled out—every other part of their name was an initial. I have seen locations where census takers used initials for non-English names instead of trying to spell them correctly. Maybe your ancestor was enumerated as J. Smith in the 1860 census. Now there's a real problem.

## Do You Know What You are Searching?

*21 December 2008*

Do not mindlessly type names in database search boxes without first learning what you are actually searching and what records and sources the database contains. Is it a website that contains voluntary submissions of data other researchers have compiled? If so, it may be incomplete. Is it an official archives site that theoretically includes every record created in a certain set of records? Even those databases may have omissions because some records were not extant or somehow overlooked. Most sites will indicate where they obtained their information (start reading the "Frequently Asked Questions," "More About" or similarly named page). Find out what was used and find if all records were extracted. Don't assume you know what is in the database. Not knowing what you are searching may explain why you are not finding the information you seek.

## Official Does not Mean Accurate

*22 December 2008*

Just because a record is "official" does not mean that every detail it contains is correct. A death certificate probably has the date of death and burial correct, but the date and place of birth could easily be incorrect depending upon the informant and their likely knowledge of the event. And there is always the less likely possibility that a death record has the wrong date of death or place of burial. An official record does not guarantee the information is accurate. Remember that in most situations, the information on a record is only as accurate as the informant. Information submitted came from someone's mind and may not have been verified with another source or official record.

## Use the Census as a Springboard

*23 December 2008*

Before interviewing relatives who were alive at the time of the 1940 census, try locating them in that record. Use their enumeration as a starting point for questions to ask. Anything in their family's enumeration can be something to ask about—even seemingly innocent details can spur a longer conversation. Note the names of neighbors and ask your relative about these individuals. Giving your interviewee specific names may help to prompt memories and get them to recall events they might not otherwise have thought about. This is helpful even if the person was not alive in 1940. Neighbors might have been neighbors for decades and even if the person did not know the former neighbors personally just hearing their name may trigger details.

## Wait to Cross the Pond

*24 December 2008*

Some genealogists are anxious to begin their foreign research as soon as they learn they have an ancestor born in a foreign country.

That's not the best way to approach an immigrant ancestor. The results may be searching in the wrong place, claiming the wrong immigrant as your own, or lacking adequate information to perform your search "across the pond." Research the ancestor in the area of settlement first as completely as possible (everywhere they lived, not just where they finally settled). Doing so may provide more detailed information about his or her geographic origins and may also provide the names of other relatives or associates whose overseas origins may be easier to trace.

## Getting Guardianships?

*26 December 2008*

Did your ancestor die with minor children? If so, there might be guardianship records for his children, particularly if he left behind real estate or a significant amount of personal property. For much of American history, women had no property rights and a widow might not be able to receive money for her children or to manage real estate they inherited from a deceased father or grandparent without being appointed as their guardian by a court. Often it was not the widow who was even appointed guardian of the children's inheritance, although she typically was automatically the guardian of the child's person.  Guardians typically had some relationship to the child—it just may not be stated in the records. The guardianship might provide more information on the children, names of potential relatives, and clues to the mother's possible remarriage. Researchers should always research the guardians fully to determine if they had any relationship to the children—either by birth or by marriage.

## Lining Out Your Research

*27 December 2008*

Do you know where all the lines are on the map of your ancestor's neighborhood? Property lines, county lines, and state lines can all play a role in your family history research. These lines changed over time as new territories were created, county lines were debated and finalized, as your ancestor bought and sold property, as your ancestor moved, etc. Contemporary and modern maps are both necessary. Local libraries and historical/genealogical societies are great places to start inquiring about the availability of such maps. Do not research your ancestor by relying solely on maps created a hundred years after her death.

## Estate Accountings of Money

*28 December 2008*

Many times, genealogists look for a will of an ancestor and stop there—especially if they find it. There may be more. Records of financial accountings and how money was actually disbursed among family members may clarify relationships that are stated vaguely in a will. Make certain you have seen all the estate papers that were created during the settlement process. If the probate of the will extends for several years, initial beneficiaries may die before the estate is closed and their own heirs may be listed in a final accounting. Specific amounts of money handed out may (or may not) clearly indicate family relationships. There's one last benefit of relatives dying with money: people tend to "reappear" when money is involved—even those who have been missing for decades. The accounting of the estate may reference individuals who you thought were lost for good.

## Did Your Ancestor Just Lie?

*29 December 2008*

If some piece of information given by your ancestor in a record does not make sense, consider the possibility that he lied. People lied for many reasons, including wanting to get married, wanting to enlist in the service, wanting to avoid the service, trying to escape their past (parents, spouse, children, debts), etc. An outright lie can be difficult to research around when there are no other clues, making it extremely important to obtain as many records on the lying ancestor as possible.

## Obituaries are not Always Correct

*01 January 2009*

Information in obituaries is often submitted by relatives at a stressful time in their lives (because their relative just died, they may be fighting with other family members, the newspaper or mortician as a "deadline," etc.). As such, these write-ups can easily contain errors or omissions. Sometimes they are intentional and sometimes they are accidental. Regardless of the reason, care must be taken when using this information. The surviving spouse might not be the parent of all the children listed. Children and stepchildren may be intermingled. Grandchildren and step-grandchildren may be intermingled as well. Numbers of grandchildren or great-grandchildren may be incorrect. Marriages may be omitted—especially if they produced no children or if there were "issues."

An uncle of mine died a few years ago. He and his first wife divorced. She was not mentioned in the obituary, nor were their three children. His second wife, however, was mentioned, as were their three daughters. Their son was not included in the obituary because he and his mother were on the "outs" at the time of the father's death. Obituaries are clues. Treat them as such. If you are looking for gospel truth, try the Bible. You might even find a few old obituaries tucked in there as well.

## Ask Permission before Posting

*02 January 2009*

Several years ago, I sent transcriptions of documents to a distant relative. She posted them online. Her online posting contained a footer saying the transcriptions were copyrighted by her and couldn't be used, transmitted, etc. by anyone else without permission. The problem was that they were not her transcriptions. They were mine because they included the unintentional errors I made when I transcribed the documents at the age of fifteen. The chance she made the exact same careless errors I did is extremely small. I'm all for copyright protection, but don't claim copyright to something someone else sends you. I am all for sharing and do it regularly myself. But if you take what I share with you, claim it is yours, and claim copyright to it, we are done sharing.

## Are You Checking the Dates?

*03 January 2009*

Always make certain you have the dates correct. Don't rely on your memory. An attendee at a computer workshop wanted me to help them locate an ancestor in the 1880 census. He gave me her name, date of birth, and family information. We spent about ten unsuccessful minutes getting creative with search techniques when I asked him if he had any other information about the ancestor. The gentleman told me he had the ancestor's obituary. Reading it, I knew why we had not found her in the 1880 census. She had already died when the census was taken. The obituary indicated she had died in 1873. Make certain the date span of the record fits your ancestor's lifespan or chronology, otherwise you may be wasting your time.

Mimka and Tjode (Goldenstein) Habben

taken probably 1907

Carthage, Hancock County, Illinois

# Chapter 2: Grains of Truth, Reversed Names, and Date Fudging

## Late Does not Mean Dead

*04 January 2009*

Remember that the use of the word "late" on a document does not necessarily mean that the person was dead when the document was created. In many legal documents, the use of the word late only indicates that the person was formerly of that location. The phrase "John DeMoss, late of Harford County, Maryland," means that John DeMoss used to live in Harford County, Maryland, and now lives elsewhere. Of course, he could be dead, but not necessarily.

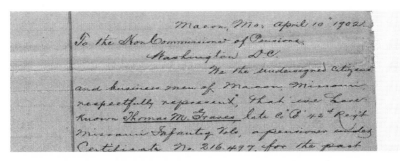

A 1902 letter to the United States Commissioner of Pensions stated that Thomas M. Graves was "late [of] Co. B 42nd Reg't Missouri Infantry Vols." This simply means that he formerly was in that company and not that he was dead in 1902

## What is a Witness?

*05 January 2009*

State statute determines who can be a witness to a legal document, but there are some general tendencies of which genealogists need to be aware. A witness to a document needs to be of sound mind and of legal age. They also should have no direct interest in the document. For example, an heir to a will should not be a witness to that will, nor should the grantor or grantee on a deed. Sometimes, one will hear that one witness was from the wife's side of the family and one was from the husband's side of the family, etc. There may be times where that happens, but it is not a hard and fast rule. A witness is only essentially saying that "I saw you sign that document and I know you are who you say you are." That's it. Of course, witnesses to a wedding may be relatives, and one may be a relative of the groom and one may be a relative of the bride. And, of course, the brother of a man may witness his will, as long as the brother is not a legatee or an heir—which he is not if the man writing the will has children of his own and is not giving the brother any property. A witness is only saying, "I saw you make your mark or sign that paper."

## Where Could the Obituary be?

*06 January 2009*

Genealogists frequently look for an obituary or death notice in the newspaper nearest to where their relative died. That is a good place to start, but the search should not end there, even if the obituary is found. Other newspapers may have carried the obituary and those write-ups might be different from the one published in the nearest town. I always check the county seat newspapers as well—whether or not the relative lived there. These newspapers might have published death notices or longer obituaries for residents throughout the county, not just residents near the county seat.

Larger towns in nearby counties might have published notices of your ancestor's death as well. Samuel Neill died in West Point, Hancock County, Illinois, in 1912. The newspaper in Carthage, the county seat, published an obituary. A newspaper in Quincy located even further away in a different county published a slightly different obituary. There could be additional ones in the smaller papers between the two towns and one of those could have an additional statement not in the two I have already located. I guess I have even more work to do!

## Tracking the Source

*07 January 2009*

Not all records or sources are created equally. That is why knowing where you obtained something is crucial. If you have a copy of great-great-grandfather's deed, is it:

- the original which passed down through the family?
- a copy of the official record at the courthouse? (which is a transcription of the original)
- a copy of a copy a relative made?
- a copy from a microfilmed copy of the original?

Perhaps the copy in the courthouse had some notation in the margin in an ink which did not show up on the microfilm. Perhaps the courthouse transcription (also known as the "record copy") contains an error. The courthouse transcription does not contain the actual signature of the individuals, just the clerk's rendition of those signatures. And on it goes. We could pontificate on citation for a long time, but I won't (at least not here). Suffice it to say that not all copies of a record are created equally, and that a complete citation should get you back to the material you copied or transcribed so that you know which version of the record you used. Then if a more complete copy becomes available, you might want to obtain it.

# Family Traditions May Have a Grain of Truth

*08 January 2009*

Some genealogists throw out an entire family tradition when part of it sounds far-fetched. While stories passed down from generation to generation may be exaggerated and Grandpa's own personal tall tale may seem like pure fantasy, there could be an iota of truth to the story. The difficulty is separating the iota of truth from the layers of incorrect detail that have been plastered over it. An ancestor's grand story of military service and a lengthy and esteemed career may really have stemmed from the fact that he was a private who saw little in the way of actual warfare. A relative supposedly living on the castle grounds may turn out to have been one who lived within sight of the castle. Include family traditions in your genealogy, but clearly label them as tradition. Even the tall tales tell something about your family. And look at the tradition closely. Could there be a nugget of truth hiding under tons of dirt?

## Names Reversed

*10 January 2009*

If you are looking for someone in the census and cannot find them, try reversing the first and last name. Perhaps the census taker did not know which name was the first name and which name was the last name. This problem can be compounded if the names are in a foreign language.

## Is a Title Mixed Up in the Name?

*11 January 2009*

An ancestor of mine was John Rucker. In some records he is listed as "Captain John Rucker." In some cases, "captain" ends up being his first name and John is his middle name. Sometimes he is simply "Captain Rucker," which makes it difficult to know if the reference is actually to John Rucker or to another Rucker man. These naming variances make a difference in how his name appears in an index or an online database. Did your ancestor have a title? Is it making him difficult or impossible to find?

## Fudging Dates?

*12 January 2009*

Always prove (if possible) dates of events given to you by family members, especially those for early generations of the family. No matter how well-meaning or cordial your relative was (or how much you love them dearly), the dates they gave you may be incorrect. One common reason for fudging dates is to make the first child arrive at least nine months after the marriage. One family history had my great-grandparents married a year earlier than they were to better "fit" the birth of their first child (the month and date were the same, just the year had been changed). In another family, the birth date of the oldest child was modified to make the first child born a year after the marriage. It is important to be accurate and not to judge. Also contemplate whether it's worth damage to a relationship with a close family member just to tell them that their information is wrong. It is important to remember that our ancestors were human. After all, if they weren't. . . what's that make us?

## Read a How-to Book or Research Guide?

*13 January 2009*

When was the last time you read a research guide or how-to book about genealogy, an area, or a time period where you are researching? It is easy for even the most experienced researcher to occasionally overlook a record type or not be aware of a record that has recently become more accessible. Periodically review a chapter in a guidebook. *The Source: A Guidebook of American Genealogy* (Third Edition) and Val Greenwood's *The Researcher's Guide to American Genealogy* (4th edition) are two of my favorites. We all need a refresher every so often. I've even been known to read a chapter from one of them when I was in need of an article idea and behind on a deadline.

## Lost Grandma or Grandpa?

*14 January 2009*

If Grandma or Grandpa "evaporates" after the death of their spouse, make certain you have searched for all their children, not just the one who is your direct line. Your ancestor could easily have moved in with any one of their adult children after the death of their spouse. Find all the children of your ancestor. Look for them in census records and expand your search from there. In pre-1850 censuses, Grandma or Grandpa may appear as a "tick mark" in one of the older columns. Grandma or Grandpa may also appear in the cemetery in a permanent place next to one of those children. If they moved several states away to live with a child, they might not have been taken "home" for burial, and husband and wife could be buried several states from each other—especially if all children had moved away.

## Identify People on Pictures

*15 January 2009*

Do you have pictures with individuals who are not identified? Work on locating someone who might be able to help you name those people, and remember that someone who may know may not be an immediate family member. The courthouse, cemetery, and library will still be around in a month (hopefully). Great aunt Myrtle might be the only one who knows who "those old people" are and her memory (or even yours) could be taken away in a moment.

## Re-Read What You Already Have

*17 January 2009*

Sometimes a clue is not a clue the first time you see it. I had used a deed as a sample in my early years of teaching genealogy classes. After a few years, I switched it out in place of a different example.

Several years later, I switched back to the earlier example, not really reading the names, but just putting it in as a sample for the legal verbiage. I read the names of the buyer and seller as I lectured about it and then I stopped. The purchaser of the land in question was an ancestor—the reason I had copied it. Now years later, I stopped and looked at the name of the seller. It was my ancestor's first cousin who had "evaporated" in Ohio and could not be located. Here he was in Illinois selling land to my ancestor. Now I know to look closely at all the names on any deed where an ancestor buys or sells property. I didn't know that when I was starting my research and originally located the record. The name of the cousin meant nothing to me at the time. How many things did you find early in your research that have not been re-analyzed?

## Have You Researched All Your Ancestor's Marriages?

*17 January 2009*

Most of us have at least one ancestor who was married more than once. Normally we do not descend from each of their spouses and the tendency is to focus on the spouse from which we do descend, particularly if the other marriage is a short one later in the ancestor's life. That can be a mistake as there can be clues to our ancestor's origins (or the first spouse's family) in that later marriage.

Archibald Kile was married three times. The first was in the 1830s in Ohio to the woman with whom he had all his children. He married twice in Illinois, both times when he was in his 70s. Searching the records of these marriages located marriage applications for him which provided the names of Archibald's parents. If I had not located the second and third marriages of this ancestor, I would have missed a great place to learn about his parents.

## No Probate? Look for a Quit Claim Deed

*18 January 2009*

Have you looked for a relative's probate file only to not find it? Are you certain that he or she owned land when they died? If you are, look for a quit claim type of deed drawn up after their death where the heirs either sell the property to another heir. It may be that your ancestor's estate "avoided" a probate filing by use of one of these deeds. Sometimes these records will say the name of the deceased owner and sometimes they do not. Consequently, to find these records, look in land indexes for the names of all known heirs of the relative whose probate you cannot find. It could easily be indexed under any of their names.

## Did Your Ancestor Even Understand What They Were Doing?

*21 January 2009*

I was at the recent annual meeting of our church congregation. A somewhat controversial matter came up, and a member called for a secret vote. We had no ballots ready, and in haste, used scratch paper made from election ballots from the previous year's election of officers. Voting members were told to write "yes" or "no" on the blank side of the paper. Despite repeating the instructions several times, several members put marks by the names of the previous year's officer candidates. It was clear they were confused. Was your ancestor confused when the census taker came to his door? Was she confused when she was asked questions about her husband's death certificate? We sometimes assume our ancestor completely understood the questions he was asked. Perhaps he was completely confused and in his confusion his answers have left us completely confused as well.

## Do You Have the Right Name?

*22 January 2009*

One of my "spare time" activities is finding well-known individuals in United States census records. There are several potential difficulties I face when trying to locate any of these individuals. One of the most common is using their birth name instead of their stage name. While most of us are not searching for celebrities in the census, it still pays to have the correct name. If grandfather was an immigrant, are we searching for both his birth name and his Anglicized name? Was there another name he took after he immigrated, perhaps one that was easier to spell or pronounce? And is the name we have for Grandma actually her middle name and not her first name? Is she enumerated under her first name in 1900, a name that perhaps we do not know, while other enumerations list her with her middle name? And there is always the chance that our ancestor changed his name to escape the law, a creditor, or a former wife.

## Will Pencil and Paper do?

*23 January 2009*

There are times when I need to chart out relationships within a family—without printing the entire tree or even the entire family group. I just need a few people. And sometimes figuring out how to do that on a computer takes up too much time, particularly when the chart is only to keep me and my research organized. A pencil and paper gets the job done faster so I can get to actual research. There are other times where actually just "scratching" things out on paper is faster. Do you need a computer for every task? Is there something you could do on paper in five minutes that would take you five hours on the computer? Remember that you are not always creating layout for a magazine or publication. Sometimes you are just making a working chart for yourself and your own use. And it saves time for research. Isn't that what it is about?

## Looking Through 21st-Century Glasses?

*26 January 2009*

When interpreting a deceased ancestor or relative's actions, consider that they probably operated from a slightly different perspective than you. There are several important things to consider about your ancestor when trying to figure out what he or she did or why he or she acted in a given way. What was your ancestor's educational level? What was his or her economic status at that point in time? What were their family obligations at that point in time? Was the ancestor isolated from relatives or did she have local family she could go to for help? Was your ancestor widowed with three children and no means of support? Did your ancestor have psychological or emotional problems? Was there a substance abuse problem? Was your ancestor hiding something? How much do you know about your ancestor's "context?" Keep in mind that you descend from your ancestor, but you are not your ancestor. Put yourself in their shoes. Take off your socks if necessary!

## Recording the Execution

*27 January 2009*

There is a difference between the date a document is executed and the date it is recorded. The date a document is executed is usually the day it is signed and becomes effective. The date of recording is the date the document is recorded officially at the courthouse. Documents cannot be recorded before they are executed, but there is often no law that deeds had to be recorded within a specific time frame. Registering vital events is different and there's usually a time frame for their registration. Wills also have to be filed for probate within a time line set by state statute. Deeds may be recorded years after they are written. This is more likely to happen if a family goes to sell a piece of property and realizes the deceased owner never had his or her original deed recorded. In those cases, you may find the deed of purchase recorded right before the deed of sale.

## Is Your Reasoning in Your Notes?

*31 January 2009*

Did you do any thinking to reach that genealogical conclusion about a parentage or a date? Hopefully at least some thinking was done before a conclusion was reached. Did you analyze several documents to reach a decision about what those documents suggested when they were analyzed together? If so, is that chain of thought somewhere in your database? Human memories are particularly frail and writing your thought process out somewhere increases the chance your logic and analysis gets preserved. It is even possible that you could later realize you were wrong. It is hard to see an error in your line of thought if it was never written down anywhere. You can put your analysis in the notes section of your genealogical software, a word processing document in with your genealogical images, or other places. But do record that process.

## What Brought Them?

*01 February 2009*

I am a big believer in studying the reasons behind an individual or a family's migration over time. Your ancestor most likely did not just arbitrarily move from point A to point B. Chances are someone encouraged him to move, sent him a letter telling him how good it was in the new area, etc. Even if there was not someone from "home" living in his new destination when he arrived, chances are someone from "home" came out to settle where he did after he was there. My wife and I have over twenty ancestral families who came from Europe in the mid-19th century. All of them settled where they already knew someone, where others from the same region had already settled, or had someone they sent for after they arrived. Even individuals travelling across the country often moved as a part of a larger group with social, ethnic, religious, or other ties. Studying these migration flows has been very informative for my research. What or who brought your ancestor from Point A to Point

B? Take the time to find out. You might learn more about history and your ancestor than you think.

## Get Out of Your Comfort Zone II

*02 February 2009*

Are you only using certain records in your search? Are there sources you do not use because you think they are too difficult to use or because you are unfamiliar with them? If so, you may be limiting the amount of information you find and leaving a significant part of your ancestor's story untold. Ignoring deeds if your ancestors were farmers is a mistake, land records may provide migration and other clues not evidenced in other records. Even city dwellers might have owned a small city lot and how that lot was dealt with after the owner's death could provide you with valuable information. And assuming your ancestors weren't the kind of people to end up in court records is a bad one to make. Many researchers also ignore court records because they are "confusing." Sometimes they do require some time to analyze, but it often can be worth it. Over half of my great-great-grandparents were involved in some type of legal action. Ignorance may be bliss, but it may also cause you to miss things in your research.

## Transcribe Those Digital Images

*04 February 2009*

No doubt a good digital image is a great rendering of a document that may be difficult to read. However, it still is to your advantage to transcribe digital copies of original records. Transcribing a document forces you to look at every word, perhaps a word you overlooked in quickly reading the document is crucial to its analysis. There are still times where sharing a typed-up transcription may be easier than sharing an image. Transcribed copies can be searched for specific words—digital images usually cannot. When you type that document, think about what every word means. Think about what every phrase means. There may be a term upon which your research may hinge. And when you do not know what a word means, look it up. It may make all the difference.

## Look for a Partition

*05 February 2009*

If you cannot find deeds or records of an estate settlement for your ancestor, look for a partition suit. These suits were usually filed when the heirs could not agree on how a farm or piece of real estate could be equitably partitioned into individual pieces amongst the heirs. These court cases will be filed in the county courthouse with other local court records—usually in a court that hears equity-type cases. The records in these cases may show (usually briefly) how the deceased obtained their property, when they died (or at least a "dead by" date), and who their heirs were. There may be a map of how the property was partitioned out if that was possible or details of the auction if it could not. All are good clues for the genealogist. I always look for partitions, but they can be particularly interesting if a relative died with no descendants. That's when all the relatives come out of the woodwork.

## Should You Import Data from Online Trees into Your File?

*06 February 2009*

It can be so tempting. A search for your ancestor on a website provides his ancestry back five generations. There it is, all compiled and easily downloadable in a file that can be imported into your own database. Should you incorporate this data willy-nilly into your database *sans* analysis? In a word, no. I use these files as clues, not as facts. If I import someone's information into my file, separating the information out later is nearly impossible. Not all submitters are careful about the accuracy of their information. Just this week, I found an online compilation with the ancestors of a first cousin of my great-grandmother. This compilation contained people dying before they had children, parents with birthdates after their children died, and ancestors who trotted the globe having children in several states and foreign countries. While this example may be extreme, it still makes the point that integrating someone else's data into ours may end in more of a mess than we had in the first place.

## Is the Database Complete?

*07 February 2009*

Some online databases are "works in progress." *Ancestry.com*, *FamilySearch*, and other sites offer some wonderful data, but some databases are not complete before they are posted. Usually this information is somewhere on the site, but it may not be obvious initially and sometimes it is not obvious at all. Make certain you know how complete something is. It still may be worth your time to search it.  But if you don't know how complete it is, you really don't know what you searched and what you didn't.

## Review Your Early Findings

*08 February 2009*

Have you reviewed information you found early in your research? Perhaps you entered data without really analyzing it or copied only parts of a document or a book without realizing that there was more. Are there any conclusions you reached early in your research that you are "sticking" to, even though you should go back and analyze them now that you know more about your family and (hopefully) about research? I have copies of court records in my files, where I now realize that I only copied part of the record because I "didn't need the rest."  Now I realize that there might be more and that there could be clues in "the rest." If you have not done it, it may be worth your time to revisit some things you "discovered" when you first started.

## Update Your Old Message Board Posts

*09 February 2009*

If you posted to the message boards at Ancestry/Rootsweb (boards.ancestry.com) or other genealogy sites, have you looked at your message lately to see if there are responses? Remember that even if a site allows you to be notified of a response, that response might have gotten stuck in your spam filter or was something you completely ignored. Also, some users don't view the "old" posts because they are concerned that the emails are out of date, etc. Consider re-posting messages to boards with updates in your information, etc., and make certain your access information is current. New people are getting into genealogy every day and someone may stumble on your old post.

## Look for Divorce or Separate Maintenance

*10 February 2009*

Don't assume that "our family" never had any divorces. Married couples have had difficulty getting along since marriage began and couples have been having difficulty getting along since forever. Information about a divorce is not one of those things that gets passed down in some families. It is easier to let the story fade into the past particularly if the marriage results in no children or if there's a very small child with no memory of the biological parent and a quick subsequent marriage. My third great-grandmother was divorced twice—from the same man. Her marriage (singular) was all the information that was passed down to later family members, likely because it resulted in four children. My great-uncle was divorced from his wife after a ten-year marriage and died a year later in an accident. There were no children and his divorce was never mentioned to later family members. His marital status was stated correctly on his death certificate.

Divorce records are usually kept with the county court records and are usually public records. The information may vary, but the date and place of marriage may be given along with names and ages of minor children. Even a divorce record on an uncle or aunt may provide testimony from their siblings or clues as to where the family lived previously.

## Grantor versus Grantee

*14 February 2009*

Do you know what the difference is between a grantor and a grantee on a land record? A grantor is someone who is selling or transferring their ownership in real property to someone else, while a grantee is someone who is purchasing property or is having property ownership transferred to them. One joke I make during lectures is about the genealogist who spent hours looking for a deed when her ancestor purchased land. Her time was spent looking in the grantor indexes. Of course, looking for when her ancestor purchased land should be done in the grantee indexes. It can be easy to get the two terms mixed up. Make certain you are looking in the right index.

## Are You Looking at What is Missing?

*15 February 2009*

Are there time periods in your ancestor's life that are not accounted for? What was he or she doing during those periods? Where was he or she living? The first five years of my ancestor's life in the United States were a complete mystery to me. John Ufkes came to the United States in the spring of 1869, settling in Illinois. He cannot be found in the 1870 census and there is no record of him until his marriage in 1874. His life is well documented from then until his death in 1924. There are a variety of land, court, census, church, and other records on a regular basis mentioning him in Adams and Hancock County, Illinois. I realize five years is not a long time in the life of an adult, but the gap always bugged me as from his marriage until his death he appears in something every few years (particularly tax records after he purchased property). Since the time period was short and other research items were more pressing, I really never worked on those five years, but they were still in the back of my mind. It turned out that John had an incomplete homestead claim in Franklin County, Nebraska, that he filed in the early 1870s. That explained his absence from Illinois records during that time period.

## Does it Make Sense?

*15 February 2009*

Before I say this, let me say that copying someone else's data into your database is not advised at all. But at least make certain it makes sense before entering it into your database. I saw an online family tree where the mother and father died before their children were born and another couple who had their children before they (the parents) were born. Woah! And if your database indicates someone died in 1742 and served in the American Revolution, something is decidedly amiss.

## Do you Understand the Index?

*17 February 2009*

Indexes to courthouse records are not always strictly alphabetical. Sometimes they are indexed by only the first letter of the last name. Some indexes are partially by last name and then by first name. The "Mc" and "Mac" names can be at the front or the end of the "M" section. Not every party in a lawsuit appears in the defendant or plaintiff index (often it is only the first defendant who appears in the defendants' index and only the first plaintiff who appears in the plaintiffs' index). Indexes can be incorrect or missing for certain volumes. Courthouses may have indexes to records that were not filmed or digitized by the Family History Library. A good idea is to ask a local person from the area who is familiar with the local records. These people can be an excellent resource as every courthouse has their own nuances.

## Does the Family History Library Have Everything?

*17 February 2009*

In a word, no. Salt Lake City's Family History Library
(www.familysearch.org) is a wonderful library in which to research.
Their collection of genealogy materials is the largest in the world,
but remember that they do not have everything that was ever
created. For many Illinois counties, the Family History Library does
not have personal property tax records from the mid-nineteenth
century and later. There are many states in the western part of the
United States where many records have not been filmed. There are
other counties where court case packets have not been filmed and
where tract indexes to land records are still accessible only at the
courthouse. The Family History Library is an excellent place to work
on your research, but do not assume that because you have
searched there that you have accessed everything. You haven't.

## Could it Be in Another Place?

*18 February 2009*

Official or unofficial copies of documents may be located in places
where you might not think to look. My ancestor's declaration of
intention from Illinois is contained in his Nebraska homestead
application since he had to document his citizenship to apply for his
homestead. Chicago voter's registrations give years and places of
naturalization for those registered voters who were not native-born
citizens. Widow's applications for a military pension may contain
certified copies of their marriage records. A cousin who got married
in Illinois and divorced in Florida filed a copy of his Florida divorce
decree in the Illinois county where he was married. And the list
goes on. Where might your ancestor have had to record a copy of a
document? It might not be in a place where you think.

## Do You Need to Research the In-Laws?

*19 February 2009*

Sometimes a researcher is tempted to ignore the "in-laws" or "step" relatives because they are not "really relatives." However, this can be a big mistake. Your biological relatives interacted quite a bit with these individuals and there is a chance a record on them could provide information on your ancestor. It is always possible that these individuals knew your ancestor long before they became related by marriage. Your ancestors did not live in complete isolation. Researching their close acquaintances may provide information on your direct line ancestors.

## Pause and Reflect for just a Minute

*22 February 2009*

Think for just a minute before making that post to a mailing list or asking that question to a friend. Is there a chance you are overlooking something obvious? It is also good to give yourself some time to let a conclusion "sit" in your mind before publishing it or posting it. Sometimes our first, "off the cuff" reactions are correct and sometimes they aren't. Haste may cause you to create a brick wall where none existed. I almost assumed a relative had military service based upon his World War II era classification record. Turns out that the classification he received meant something different during war time than during peace time and the chart of classifications I was using were peace time classifications. When I looked at the appropriate set of classifications, what I thought was unusual was not. Sometimes a little reflection answers our questions, and it always helps to ask when you are confused. It can be better to ask when you think you are not confused just in case what you think is correct is not.

## Go Back and Browse

*24 February 2009*

With more and more records being indexed and more genealogists relying on online finding aids, it is tempting for some to quit searching when the index fails. Keep in mind that there are times where manual searching of a record is necessary. Indexes are not perfect and sometimes writing is extremely difficult to read. The census is a good example. If you know where your ancestor lived and the index does not quickly locate him, search manually. If the relative was in a rural area, it may not take very long to page through a township or two in an attempt to find him. And in searching page by page, you may find other relatives in the process. In urban areas, you may be able to pinpoint your relative's location down to a handful of enumeration districts. And learning more about where your ancestor lived and tracking his residences may help you research more than just locating him in the census. Those of us who researched in the days before census indexes relied on manual searches when we first started.

## Did You Jump to a Conclusion?

*26 February 2009*

It has been about ten years, but there used to be a local band named "DOS GUYS." There were three ways one could take this:

- DOS Guys meaning 2 guys from "dos," Spanish for two.
- DOS Guys as a way of saying "those" guys, "dos" as a slang way of saying "those."
- DOS Guys, meaning guys who were still using the DOS operating system on their computer.

Is there something that could be interpreted more than one way? Have you "jumped" on one interpretation that may be the wrong one? It may be that you are creating your own brick wall by doing so.

## Remember They Are Transcriptions

*26 February 2009*

Many pre-1920 deeds or wills contained in a record book at the courthouse is not the original and is a transcription (frequently handwritten or typed) of the original item. The grantee got the original deed and the courthouse had the transcription. As technology developed, microfilm copies, various photographic reproductions, and other kinds of copies were made. But that deed from 1850 you found in a book with all the others was a handwritten copy of the original and could contain an error or two although most clerks were fairly conscientious about copying these records as they were legal equivalents of the original. Wills recorded in a will record book are the same way. Of course, the original will may be in the packet of estate papers or otherwise filed in the local records office, but anything "recorded" before photocopies and the like was a handwritten transcription created by hand and not machine. Just a little something to keep in mind the next time you make a copy of a will from 1820.

*Nancy Jane (Newman) Rampley,
1846-1923, probably taken
Hancock County, Illinois.*

# Chapter 3: Links, Cutting off, Soundex, Perspective, and Infants

## Every Link in the Chain

*27 February 2009*

Make certain you really research from the most recent and work your way to earlier events. For years, I assumed (incorrectly) that an uncle by marriage was only married one time—to my ancestor's sister. Turns out his wife had died young and the uncle remarried shortly after her death. The woman he had children with was actually his second wife and not my aunt. The problem was exacerbated by the fact that the first marriage took place after the 1880 census and no vital records were kept and both wives were dead by the 1900 census.

## Can You Take Your Cell Phone in the Courthouse?

*28 February 2009*

Find out the security policy of the courthouse before you make a trip there. I am in the habit of sometimes making notes about what to research in the notepad feature of my phone and using my phone as a research assistant. Some courthouses will not let you bring your cell phone into the building for any reason. Find out about any security issues before you make a trip to any courthouse, especially one that is a distance from your home. It is also a good idea to find out what kinds of electronic equipment generally are allowed in the records area and research rooms. Best not to find out about restrictions at the last minute.

## Exhaust One Place Before You Venture Out

*02 March 2009*

I was researching a relative in Champaign County, Illinois. A local library had a vertical file on the family which contained a death notice from an undated, unsourced newspaper that indicated the relative was killed by a train. The only problem was that the newspaper clipping was a photocopy of the original. There was no reverse side I could look at for clues. The only geographic location mentioned in the clipping was the state of Indiana—nothing more specific. Then I remembered the deceased had an interest in an estate in the Illinois county where he lived. The probate records of that county contained a packet of his estate papers. That packet contained a transcription of the coroner's report from the county where he died in Indiana. Problem solved without looking in one Indiana county after another. You can't solve every problem this way, but exhausting all sources in the area combined with asking yourself, "what are all the records this event could have generated?" are often a good way to start.

## Another Reason to Search Every Record

*03 March 2009*

Sometimes we can be tempted to not look at every record, thinking that we do not need it or that the information it probably provides will only be the same as information we already have. After all, why do we need a different document that says what we already know? Because that additional source may have a different informant and confirm what we know or indicate that we do not know everything that we think we do. Once I almost neglected locating a 1930 census entry for a family because "I didn't need it." Turns out I was wrong. It listed the "birth" name for a daughter, which ended up being a clue as to the name of the father's mother. You just never know. And don't assume that you do not need a record just because you "know everything."

## Read and Review

*04 March 2009*

There is a "game" going around on Facebook where you pick the book nearest to you and type in the fifth full sentence on page fifty-six. I learned something when I did it. The book I grabbed was Echo King's *Finding Answers in British Isles Census Records*. King mentioned that in the 1841 UK Census enumerators were not required to give full Christian names of enumerees. I probably knew this at one point in time, but it did not hurt me to be reminded. While I'm not going to spend all day randomly picking out random pages from random books to read, the exercise did remind me that every so often it is a good idea to look at one of those references we have not read in a while and review a chapter or two. We may learn something. I know I did.

## Look at More than One Newspaper

*06 March 2009*

Do not limit your search for obituaries to just one newspaper. Your search may start with the newspaper closest to where your ancestor lived or died (a good and reasonable idea), but it should not end there. If your ancestor lived in an urban area, consider looking at other papers for that city or suburban newspapers near where the ancestor lived. If your ancestor was in a rural area, look at nearby papers and always look at the newspaper from the county seat. If your ancestor was an immigrant or the child of immigrants, consider searching for foreign language or ethnic newspapers that catered to members of that ethnic group or speakers of that language. Religious or denominational newspapers may be helpful as well. Different newspapers do not always give the exact same information.

## Ask Yourself Why?

*07 March 2009*

Genealogists should be asking themselves "why?" whenever they locate a document ("why was this document created?" "What purpose did this document serve?"). Sometimes the answer is easy. Death certificates are created because someone dies, marriage certificates are created because someone was married. Of course, vital records (and some other records) are kept simply because your ancestor existed. Other records are created because your ancestor did something. Wills are recorded because someone who had written a will died and the estate needed to be settled according to the terms of the will. Guardianships are recorded usually because a parent died and left an estate and minor children. Deeds are recorded because land was sold. Sometimes deeds are recorded because the surviving spouse died and the property needed to be transferred from their ownership. Sometimes this fact will not even be indicated on the deed. It is not the document's job to tell you exactly why it was created. Researchers occasionally need to determine that themselves.

## Do You Just Need Some Advice?

*08 March 2009*

If you are stuck on an ancestor, you might consider hiring a professional genealogist to work on your problem. Sometimes this is cost prohibitive depending on the time period, details of your ancestor's life, what you already know, and your budget. Professionals do not work for free as they also have bills to pay and mouths to feed. However, some will do consulting work at a lower total cost than actually doing full-on research for you. In a consultation, they read over your organized material and make suggestions. Sometimes that is all you need—suggestions of what to do next.

I paid for a consultation recently and it was exactly what I needed—another set of eyes to look over what I had already done and located and make certain that I had not overlooked something. One warning: organize your information first. Any professional receiving unorganized information will need to organize it before they can make suggestions for further research. That takes time and increases the number of their billable hours. A plumber will charge me for his time if he spends fifteen minutes cleaning out the cabinet under the sink before he can actually do any plumbing work. It is the same when a professional genealogist must organize your information before she gets started. She needs to clean first. That's usually something you can do yourself and save a little money in the process.

## Help Someone Else?

*09 March 2009*

Have you considered helping someone else with their genealogy? I'm not suggesting spending months of intense research on one person's problem, but have you considered offering to take pictures of stones in a nearby cemetery or to perform lookups in a book you have at home? Have you answered a query on a mailing list that does not relate to one of your families? Sometimes it feels good to just help someone else with their research. Sometimes it generates good "genealogy karma." And sometimes, when you help someone else, you learn something that later helps you with your own research.

## Clean it Out?

*10 March 2009*

They put new carpet in my office at work. The drawback was that I had to take everything out of my office. The upside was I "found" folders and papers I had forgotten about or mislaid. Do you have stacks of copies in your genealogy workspace that have been neglected? Do you even know what is in those stacks? Go through and clean up your genealogy work area. At the very least you may be more efficient, at least temporarily until the stacks re-appear. You may also find something you completely forgot you ever had.

## Cut Off the Name

*12 March 2009*

Have you tried searching for that ancestral last name by cutting part of it off? Perhaps "De Moss" was entered as "Moss." Perhaps "Van der Walle" was entered as just "Wall." "Goldenstein" might have been entered as "Golden." The list goes on. Consider what might have happened if someone dropped the first syllable or two of your ancestor's last name, then try the same for the last syllable or two. You might be surprised at what you find. I've even seen Trautvetter listed as Vetter.

## Do You Know the Soundex Codes for Your Surnames?

*13 March 2009*

Many database searches allow users to perform Soundex Codes.

A Soundex searches focuses on the last name being entered. This allows users to look for names that "sound like" the name that was entered in the search box. This is great as long as you are aware of how it works and do not overlook reasonable variants of the last name in the process that Soundex does not catch. For this reason, it is good to know the Soundex codes for your last names and their variants. Not because you need them to search, but so you know what names you need to perform Soundex searches for in order to not miss any results. The last name "Demoss" occasionally gets misinterpreted as "Demop." A Soundex search for Demoss will not bring up Demop because the two are not Soundex equivalent. Demoss has a Soundex code of D520 while Demop has a Soundex code of D510.

| Name | Soundex | Name | Soundex | Name | Soundex |
|------|---------|------|---------|------|---------|
| Neal | N400 | Golden | G435 | Buller | B460 |
| Neill | N400 | Goldenstein | G435 | Bulter | B436 |
| O'Neil | O540 | Goldenstien | G435 | Butler | B346 |
| O'Neill | O540 | Goldstein | G432 | Butter | B360 |
| Nealle | N400 | Gultenstein | G453 | Beetler | B346 |

Searching for "Demoss" with Soundex turned on will not bring up any Demop references. This site will give you the Soundex code for your last names: bradandkathy.com/genealogy/yasc.html.

## Check out Your Local Library

*14 March 2009*

Does your local library have access to any fee-based databases or sites that could be helpful in your genealogical research? Many libraries subscribe to a variety of databases including digital magazines and journal articles, historical archives, etc. Not all of these are technically "genealogy," but many academic articles of a historical or sociological nature have genealogical applications. Nearby university libraries or larger regional libraries may have access to databases that smaller ones cannot afford to maintain. That's true even if those facilities don't have a genealogy collection.

## Post to the Message Boards

*15 March 2009*

Is there a brick wall you have been stuck on for a long time? Is there a message board you have not posted to about that problem? Think of the counties where the person lived and post your query to one of those boards. There are message boards at Ancestry.com (http://boards.ancestry.com) and other sites as well (*Note: Facebook groups are more popular at the time this material was edited than when it was written. Check those out as well*).

A researcher in a workshop was stuck on a family and one of my suggestions was that she post her question about the confusing deed extract to that county's message board. My hope was that a "local" would be more familiar with the nuances of local records and could help her. She got two responses. One was from a researcher of the same name and another offered to help with the extract. All within twenty-hours. No guarantees, but it might be worth a try.

## Keep Your Perspective

*17 March 2009*

Locating a divorce record gave me a new spelling for my grandmother's maiden name of Trautvetter. The new (to me) variant is "troutfitter." I performed a Google search for the spelling, finding many references that I had not encountered before. Most of the sites had to do with fishing and I was initially confused. It took me a few minutes before I realized most of the "troutfitter" references were a play on the word "trout" and "outfitter." Then it made sense, but I also realized that, for the majority of the pages I located, "troutfitter" was not based upon someone's name. Oh well. There is a world outside of genealogy. I will still look for Troutfitter (and Trautfitter) references but won't assume they all have to do with the last name, and my Google searches will be constructed to not include webpages that have references to "trout" or "fish." It's always good to add an additional variant to the list when fishing for ancestors.

## What is an Infant?

*18 March 2009*

An 1830 document indicates your ancestor is an infant and has a guardian appointed for her. The next year the ancestor marries. What gives? An "infant" in the legal sense is someone who is under the age of majority. While that age can vary from state to state and has changed over time, it typically is eighteen for females and twenty-one for males. Make certain to confirm this with state statue, applicable law, or common practice, for the time period and area in which your ancestor lived. Your ancestor could be fifteen years old and legally be an infant. Technically my ancestor could have been an infant one day and old enough to be legally married the next. Just something to keep in mind.

## What is a Homestead?

*20 March 2009*

The word homestead can mean several things depending upon the context. It could mean a "homestead" claim that was filed under the Homestead Act of 1862. These claims usually were 160 acres and in the American Great Plains and points west, but the amount of property can vary depending upon the location and time period. Claimants would be deeded the entire homestead acreage if they lived on the farm for a given number of years and improved it. A "homestead" also could be referring to that portion of a family's farm containing their actual home and surrounding buildings that often was allowed to the widow if her husband died (the details of this allowance were set by state statute). This homestead was usually protected from creditors in the event of her husband's death. Sometimes the residence and the widow's actual "dower" would be lumped together as her right of "homestead and dower." The technical definition can vary from state to state—refer to applicable state statutes for a precise definition. Note that a "homestead exemption" for various sorts of taxes is something entirely different. When "homing" in on a definition, remember that context matters.

## Drop the Last Name When Searching?

*21 March 2009*

Have you considered dropping the last name when searching for an ancestor in a census or other record? This is especially a good idea for a relative who went by three names and whose middle name closely resembles a surname. My ancestor Henry Jacobs Fecht is listed as Henry Jacobs in the 1870 census. It took me a while to find him listed like that. John Michael Trautvetter could be enumerated as first name John and last name Michael. Just something to consider if the usual search attempts do not pan out.

# Chapter 4: Contemporary, "Paper or Plastic," and Eternal Neighbors

## It Is Relative

*22 March 2009*

Never use the word "Grandma." My daughter set up "accounts" for the family to use on her laptop. One evening I needed to use the computer and I was prompted for a password. My "generic" password that I typically use did not work and upon the submission of an incorrect entry I was given a hint: "Grandma's maiden name." I immediately entered in each of my grandmother's maiden names. Once in lower case and once in upper case. I was just about to get irritated when I realized that my daughter had meant HER grandmother, not mine. Two seconds later, the password let me in. Avoid using words such as "grandma," "uncle," or "aunt" without more information when referring to individuals in notes in your genealogical database, communications with family members, etc. Grandma Neill can be confusing. After all, whose Grandma Neill is it? Records are confusing enough sometimes without us making things more vague in our comments, notes, and transcriptions.

## Are Your Maps Contemporary?

*23 March 2009*

Genealogists need maps to organize information geographically, to know where to look for records, and to have an idea of how their ancestor's residences fit into the larger area as a whole. One key is that the maps be contemporary to the ancestor's residence in the area. Modern maps can be helpful in finding current locations of cemeteries and other landmarks, but many other times our research requires contemporary maps. If you are stuck on a forebear, get maps of his or her area. Perhaps that map is just the one you need to get you around or over that brick wall. You will certainly need them if you must manually search for him in census records.

## Read the Page Before and After

*25 March 2009*

The genealogist should always be looking for more and wanting more. Whenever a relative has been located in a record, view at least the page before and after the record for your relative. This is always good advice with census records as names of neighbors could be extended family members, associates of your ancestor who migrated along with them, individuals whose names appear as witnesses on other documents, etc. If you locate a deed, view the ones recorded before and after the desired item. Sometimes people wait to record the deed of purchase until they sell the property or realize that they have other un-recorded deeds. This may also be helpful with declarations of intent to become citizens and final naturalizations. Relatives or associates may have travelled to the courthouse together to navigate the naturalization process and their records may have been filed sequentially. Births are not usually recorded together unless there was a multiple birth. Baptisms may have been recorded for the entire family as a group for one reason or another. And deaths are another story—death certificates recorded at the same time as your relative may indicate that others were dying of the same illness at the same time and that may suggest some sort of small outbreak of disease.

## Does One Letter Make a Difference?

*26 March 2009*

How would one letter change that name? The omission of one letter changes "Orange" to "range." Quite a difference. How would the omission of one letter from the surname for which you are searching change it? Would the Soundex code be the same? Would the name even be pronounced the same? Would the error be easy to find in an index? Think about one letter being dropped from a name. You might be surprised at the variants you come up with.

## "Paper or Plastic"

*26 March 2009*

It is not really a "tip," but I thought it interesting nevertheless: In a banquet speech that must have been at least ten years ago, I made the following fictional comments: "After Smithton County had their county marriage records digitized, the county board contemplated what to do with the originals. In an effort to conserve space, save money, and express concern for the environment, the Board decided to send the original paper copies of the old records to the local paper recycling center. Board President Wannabee Paula Tician commented, 'This allows us to reduce county expenses and even lets dead people help with recycling. The next time you get to choose between paper and plastic, your great-grandparents' marriage license might literally be 'in the bag.'"

Do you know what happened to the original records when the digital images or microfilm images you are using were made?

## Can You Concentrate?

*27 March 2009*

Having difficulty staying focused on your research? Perhaps working on your computer is part of the problem. Recently on a four-hour flight with no internet to keep me "constantly in touch with the world," I realized I got more work done in those four hours than I had in the previous four days. There were no instant messages, no emails, no phone calls. Admittedly, the plane was a little cramped, but not having constant distractions helped me to organize my research and decide where I could progress next. Sometimes when we get an idea about a family history problem, it is tempting to go to a website right away, do some research, and get sidetracked. The next thing you know, it is several hours later and you barely spent five minutes on what you really wanted to research.

## Before You Do Data Entry

*28 March 2009*

Some families are a little bit complicated, while others are so interconnected and full of repeated first names that sorting them out seems nearly impossible. In these situations, it can be easy to enter the incorrect relationships in our genealogical database— particularly if we perform data entry on relationships before we have done any data analysis. What I do in these situations is to map out the relationships on paper first to get a broader view of the family and in an attempt to understand the relationships correctly. Once I think I have the relationships down, I begin my data entry. Wasting time "fixing" relationship mistakes is time I could spend doing actual research.

## Spell Check Doesn't Always Work and Computers Don't Think.

*29 March 2009*

Don't rely on spell check to find all your errors. Sometimes when transcribing old documents, it is actually easier to not use the spell and grammar check—at least for me. Old documents are full of incorrect spellings, incorrect usage, and other peccadillos that send modern computer software into error-discovery overdrive. Read it and proof it for yourself. That's the best way to catch mistakes and to notice clues in the document that were overlooked when transcribing. You should also remember that your genealogy software doesn't correct your logic or fix your conclusions. It may warn you about some obvious errors, but those other errors (relationship mistakes and the like) are up to you to find.

# Is it Complete?

*30 March 2009*

Before using any online database, determine whether it is complete. Many times, vendors will release "part" of a database, hoping to generate publicity and new sales. The problem is that many times users do not read the details of the database to find out exactly what it contains. Sometimes it's necessary to actually browse the dataset to determine just what is there. Before you spend hours searching that database, determine how complete it actually is. Clever searches for an 1877 death notice will not discover it if the newspapers from 1877 have not yet been included in the set of digital images.

# Sometimes an Error is an Error

*31 March 2009*

A 1907 era court case from Illinois involves the children of my ancestor as defendants. They are all listed correctly with the right first names in virtually every court document, except one. On the deed where the judge is selling the real estate, William Rampley is listed as Wilbur Rampley. William's middle name was not Wilbur and he never used that name as a nickname. The case file of papers contains nearly fifty separate documents and Wilbur as a name is only mentioned on the one deed. What happened? Most likely a simple transcription error on the part of the clerk. When every other reference to him in the records is William and one out of fifty lists him as Wilbur, it's easy to realize that sometimes an error is just that, an error. The document is transcribed as it is written using Wilbur so that I don't lose the reference and so that the item is transcribed accurately.

The problem is that when we have just one reference to an individual it can be difficult to know if a name is simply an error or something more. Just a little something to think about. Clerks are human. They make the occasional mistake.

## Did Grandma Even Say It Right?

*02 April 2009*

Years ago, in an article, I mentioned a "birder house." It was the little shed where my Grandma Neill had kept her baby chickens after she purchased them from the hatchery. Grandma was the only person I knew who had chickens and I had heard her use the phrase since I was a small child. She always said it like "birder house," and it seemed like a logical name for a building that kept chickens because they are little birds. What she actually meant, however, was "brooder house," referring to a brood of chickens, not a "bird." Is there a name, a word, or a place name that you heard "wrong" from a relative? Many times, we don't question these interpretations, especially if it's something we've heard "forever." Is that the reason you cannot find it? Perhaps Grandma was pronouncing it in her own way or you heard it in your own way. If no one else used that pronunciation, you may have difficulty in finding the correct location. Grandma always said she was born in "Tiogee," but that's another story for another tip!

## Do You REALLY KNOW it?

*03 April 2009*

Is there something you think you know but for which you have no real proof other than you have always believed it? While it doesn't have direct genealogical bearing, I have been reading *Pillars of the Republic* by Carl F. Kaestle. One thing I learned while reading the book is that there were many schools in the 1820s-1840s that enrolled children as young as four. This trend changed in the mid-eighteenth century. I just always assumed that there was no schooling at all for children that young until the 20th century. I never read that anywhere, I just assumed it. Is there some "fact" in your genealogy research that you never read, never heard, but just assumed? And is it causing that brick wall in your research?

## They Don't Film Everything

*05 April 2009*

Just remember, even if it appears that the Family History Library has a great deal of information on your county or locality of interest, there probably are more records actually in the area that were not filmed. The Family History Library films quite a bit, but they don't always get every piece of paper in the courthouse. And some courthouses that do let them digitize materials don't let them digitize everything—only selected materials.

## Record Those Stones Now

*06 April 2009*

A few months ago, I stopped at a cemetery where several ancestors are buried. I had not been there in years. The stone whose information I had transcribed had fallen over and was not nearly as legible as it had been ten years ago. One of my summer goals is to visit every nearby ancestral cemetery and get pictures and information off those stones. One day it may be too late.

## The Fragile Human Mind

*07 April 2009*

Write down your own life story and ask those interview questions you have been putting off. The human mind is the most fragile repository we use. Don't waste it and don't miss an opportunity.

## Search Collateral Lines for Pensions

*09 April 2009*

Military pensions, especially if the widow survived and claimed a pension via her husband's service, may provide information about more than just the veteran and his widow. Relatives might have had to testify to the marriage of the veteran and his wife, their residences from the time they married until the pension was applied for, their children (particularly if any were underage), and other information necessary to document the pension. These statements are more detailed if the widow cannot find her marriage certificate or is missing other documents (bad for her, good for your research). Relatives who were present at the marriage or who knew of the couple's marriage might have signed an affidavit to that effect.  My ancestor's Civil War widow's pension provided information about the wife's family, including her siblings. She also indicated who was at her 1867 wedding and the sister-in-law who was present at the birth of one of her children.

## Nuncupative Will

*10 April 2009*

A nuncupative will is a will that is orally dictated by the testator. These are typically deathbed type wills, made at the last minute. This will is to be written down as soon as possible by the witnesses and presented to the court within the time allowed for probate. Not all jurisdictions have honored these as valid.

## Places of Birth at the Time of the Record

*11 April 2009*

Remember that places of birth as given in census and other records may have been stated as they were at the time the record was created, not the time the birth actually took place. At different times, my ancestor (born in the 1850s) indicated she was born in Prussia, Hanover, or simply Germany. This was because of who was "ruling" the village where she was born *at the time of the census or other record*. It may just seem like great-great-grandma was confused when she really was not. She was giving information that was correct as of the time she was giving it.

## Preserve Your Originals

*12 April 2009*

Never take your only copy of a document with you on a research trip. You may lose it. Never put the original copy of a document out for permanent display. Sunlight will permanently fade it. Use copies. Save yourself the pain of losing or destroying the only copy of something you have. Keep your originals safe.

## How are they Organized?

*13 April 2009*

Some records are organized geographically (census), some records are organized chronologically (vital records), and some are organized by name (indexes). Learn how a record series is organized before you use it. That will help you glean as much from it as you can.

## Get a Legal Dictionary

*14 April 2009*

For many genealogists, a legal dictionary is a great help. This is especially true when analyzing court and probate records where legal terms may be used profusely. I picked up on eBay several years ago. A current one is not necessary and may be beyond your genealogy budget. Mine dates from the 1980s and serves my purpose well. There are also digital images of out-of-copyright legal dictionaries available on sites such as *GoogleBooks* (books.google.com) and *Archive.org* (www.archive.org).

## Look at the Eternal Neighbors

*15 April 2009*

When you locate that ancestor in a cemetery, look at the neighboring stones. There is a reasonable chance they are relatives. At least copy down the names and information (or take pictures) while you have the chance. Make certain your images include the relative positions of all the stones that you have photographed individually. Five years later (when you have discovered their names in other records) it may be too late to get information from their stones.

# Chapter 5: Undoing, Discrepancies, Math, and Avoiding Court

## Review on Birthdays

*17 April 2009*

Here's an off-the-wall idea—but some days I find writing tips a little difficult. Make a calendar with your ancestor's dates of birth on it. Then on the ancestor's birthday, review the information you have about that person. This might help you find something in your files that you had forgotten or overlooked. You can choose arbitrary dates on your "review calendar" for individuals for whom you have no actual date of birth. Just never indicate that the review date is their actual date of birth.

## Learn the Foreign Language Script

*18 April 2009*

Remember that there is more to reading records in a foreign language than simply learning the vocabulary. Foreign language records are often written in a different script and that letter that looks like an "L" to the eye trained in English script may actually be a "B" if the script is from a different language. There are a variety of online sites that can provide you with the ideal way letters were to have been written. Use these as a guide as not every writer makes their letters in the "correct" way.

## Can You Undo It?

*20 April 2009*

If you have an original copy of a document or photograph, do not do anything to that paper or photograph that cannot be undone. Putting it in a frame or an envelope (usually) is one thing. Taping it in a book or gluing it to something is another.

## Using All the Indexes

*21 April 2009*

In some cases, there may be several online sites or databases that index the same set of records. Consider using other indexes when available and when one index does not help you to find the desired person. Another person making their own index may read something differently than did the first person. Don't assume someone is not in a record because one index fails to include him. Ask others if they know if there is another finding aid for the records you are searching or if there is a workaround for someone you cannot locate. Also remember that a manual search of the records may still be necessary, and your person may not be in the records you are searching. That's always a possibility as well.

## Discrepancy Charts

*22 April 2009*

Genealogy information does not always agree. It's actually more common for it to be inconsistent than it is for it to be consistent. Create a discrepancy chart including a column for the source that was used, the piece of information it gave that was inconsistent with other records, the citation for the source, the likely informant, the probable reliability of the informant, and the perceived reliability of the document. Create one row for each source. The chart won't make inconsistent information consistent, but it may help you realize if there is at least some consistency between the records or if some of them are probably more reliable than others.

## Discrepancy Chart

## Ida Mae Sargent birth date/place

| Record | Birth date | Birthplace | Age | Informant | Information Type |
|---|---|---|---|---|---|
| Son John's death certificate, 1937 | Not given | Alexandria, Clark, Missouri | Not given | | Secondary |
| Ida's death certificate, 1939 | 1 April 1874 | Adams County, Illinois | 65 years, 2 months, and 22 days | Hospital Records | Secondary |
| Ida's Obituary, 1939 | 1 April 1874 | Warsaw, Hancock, Illinois | 65 years | | Secondary |
| Marriage to George TRAUTVETTER, 1898 | Ca. 1874/1875 | Iowa | 23 years | Probably Ida | Secondary |
| Marriage to William MILLER, 1936, | Ca. 1873/1874 | Lima, Adams, Illinois | 63 years | Probably Ida | Secondary |
| 1880 Census | Ca. 1873/1874 | Iowa | 6 years | | Secondary |

# Was Grandma Mixed Up?

*23 April 2009*

Sometimes errors in genealogical records are unintentional. Census and christening records indicate my grandmother was born in Wythe Township, Hancock County, Illinois, in 1910. Grandma always thought she was born in Tioga, Hancock County, Illinois—in nearby Walker Township. On every record from her marriage through her death, Grandma's place of birth was put down as Tioga, because that is what she thought it was. The error wasn't intentional, but rather was based upon her belief as to where she was born. I have noted the discrepancy in all the records and made a note about what Grandma thought in her file so that someone else will know why there are the differences in her records. Errors happen for a variety of reasons. I was lucky in this case because I knew how the errors got there. That does not always happen.

## Doing the Math Right?

*25 April 2009*

Are you subtracting correctly when taking an age and calculating a year of birth? It might pay to double-check your computations so you do not create errors in your own records. It seems like a simple thing, but a subtraction error, especially if done in your head late at night while on the computer, can easily happen. And a year of birth calculated as 1802, when it should be 1812, might make all the difference in interpreting other records correctly.

## Read the Description

*27 April 2009*

Always make certain you read the description of a data set before searching. This allows you to see if it includes the information you need. The *FamilySearch* web site includes some Ohio Tax records. I was excited as both my wife and I have early Ohio ancestors. At the time I visited the site, only a few counties were included. I also needed to determine if the site included both real and personal property tax records, who had to pay personal property tax, etc. They will add records to the site, but reading what areas are included before I search a database saves me time if the locations I need are not yet included.  Knowing something about the records the site includes also helps me to better use the records.

## Ask for Ideas?

*28 April 2009*

Consider asking someone unrelated to your family to look at a document or a record that confuses you. Going to your local genealogical society meeting can be one way to do this. Another is to scan the document and share it with others electronically (perhaps via email, on a blog, in a Facebook group, etc.) This can be a good way to get short documents translated or at least to have someone look at a word or a phrase that is difficult to read. Sometimes it is best to have someone look at the item who is unrelated to the family, unfamiliar with them, etc. They will have a fresh perspective and won't have the assumptions about the individuals that you may have. Just make certain that they do understand genealogical records and research.

## Is There a Larger Index?

*30 April 2009*

Never let someone tell you there is no index or there is just one index to something. Determine if there is another index or if an index was created and published privately. There were a series of land records I was searching for in a county in Illinois while at the Family History Library. The land record books were indexed individually with an index at the front of each volume. What the Family History Library did not have was another index to the land records that was created and maintained at the courthouse. That index had not been filmed and consequently was not at the Family History Library. Using that index, it took me five minutes to find the deeds I needed. Going through the volumes' indexes one-by-one would have taken me significantly longer.

Of course, it is always possible that any index will miss the entry that you need. Occasionally items are overlooked when indexes are created.

# Jumping to Conclusions

*01 May 2009*

Don't jump to conclusions. Your first response to a record or a document may be incorrect. I posted to my Facebook account recently that I had been in the courtroom in the Hancock County, Illinois, courthouse in front of the judge. One can draw several conclusions from that. The reality is that I was there for a wedding. That statement really isn't clear either as it doesn't indicate whose wedding it was (hint: it was not mine). Find out more before you reach a conclusion. Don't assume. Be careful reading more into a statement than is there. It may cause you to go off on a completely incorrect research tangent. In some cases, it may even cause you to spread gossip!

# Clues in Metes and Bounds Descriptions

*02 May 2009*

Sometimes the uninitiated are not aware of the neighborhood clues that are contained in the metes and bounds property description that are typically given in local land records from state land states. These descriptions are the ones that give the boundaries of the property by listing the points, the angles, and the lengths of each side. Frequently these descriptions will mention by names the other owners of properties that border the property being transferred *(example:* "thirty rods along the line of John Rucker until it meets the line of Susannah Fields and thence sixty rods in her line…"). This can be a great way to get names of neighbors of your ancestor.

# Just Read a Newspaper

*03 May 2009*

A great way to get a perspective on your ancestor's time and place is to read an issue or two of their hometown newspaper while you are searching for that obituary or other item. In addition to the national news, there will be local news. Reading the paper will give you a history lesson in microcosm and may make you aware of things you never learned in history class. It might give you an entirely different viewpoint on your ancestor as well. And being familiar with the newspaper's layout and general style never hurt either as that often assists in manual searching of newspapers as the same type of items usually appear in the same spot in each edition.

## Occupations

*04 May 2009*

Have you tried to learn the occupations of each of your ancestors? Knowing how your ancestor supported his family may provide suggestions as to what kinds of records he may have left behind. It might also explain migration patterns, family social status, etc. And if you know what your ancestor's occupation was, have you learned about that occupation during the time he or she lived? That, too, may provide you with more insight into your ancestor's life.

## Needing a Project?

*05 May 2009*

If you need a change of pace, determine those ancestors for whom you have a copy of their signature. Remember, most recorded deeds and wills do not contain original signatures—they are the clerk's handwritten transcription of the signature that was on the deed. Some clerks will try to copy a customized mark an ancestor made—someone whose last name was DeMoss may have signed with a "D" mark instead of an "X.") Searching for signatures may cause you to locate records for which you never thought to look. Ask yourself: "what possible documents could my ancestor have actually signed?" to get yourself started.

## Base Lines and Meridians

*06 May 2009*

Need help with base lines and meridians in federal land states? These surveying reference points are often referred to in legal property descriptions in federal land states. The Bureau of Land Management website has a map of these lines at glorecords.blm.gov/images/reference/principal meridians and baselines .png. The "Reference Center" at the Bureau of Land Management website has excellent information on surveying and property descriptions federal land records as well: glorecords.blm.gov/reference/default.aspx. If you don't know the difference between a section and a township and are unaware of how many acres are in a quarter-section, this site will have relevant helpful details to assist in understanding the terminology.

## Google that Minister

*07 May 2009*

I finally located the marriage record for an ancestor of my wife. It was the first marriage for him and the one from which my wife did not descend. On a whim, I Googled the name of the minister. It turns out he was well known in his area, founded what is now a nationally known university, and was involved in many activities in the mid-nineteenth century. Also, because of Googling him, I learned the name of the church he was pastor of at the time of the marriage and found the email of the church archivist. I think I'll be Googling more minsters. I won't hit pay dirt every time, but one never knows.

## Look for the In-laws

*08 May 2009*

If your research has hit a brick wall, make certain you have completely researched the in-laws. It may be that a record on one of them provides the missing link to your direct line ancestor.

## Write it Yourself

*09 May 2009*

If you are having difficulty reading handwriting in a foreign language, after you've located a script guide, try writing it yourself. Practicing the script by using your own hand is an excellent way to "get it in your head" and can also help you notice writing irregularities that are common. It also gives you a different perspective than simply reading the writing.

## Think "Who Gave it?"

*10 May 2009*

If you are confused about a document, consider who gave the information and how they came to know that information. While your speculation may not be correct, it may get you to thinking about the perceived accuracy of the information. And that may be helpful. Also bear in mind that while one person may be listed as the informant on a record, several people may have actually been involved in the information gathering process.

## All the Cousins?

*11 May 2009*

If you are at an impasse, have you actually located all the possible relatives who might be able to help you in your search? My wife's great-grandfather "disappeared" circa 1918. I'm not certain if he was in World War I, moved away and never communicated again, etc. I do know that it is possible that a descendant of one of his five siblings might have heard what happened to him. He may even have maintained some sort of communication with one of them even if he never communicated with his children. My search for him is not complete until I have worked on locating the descendants of his siblings to see if they have additional information.

## Historical Context?

*12 May 2009*

Have you put your ancestor's life into the appropriate historical context? As mentioned in my earlier post, a relative "disappeared" circa 1918. While there are many things that could have happened to him or places he could have gone, it is always possible that he enlisted in World War I and died overseas. That would explain quite a bit about his disappearance, especially if he was estranged from his family at the time. He may not have lived to re-establish communication with them. Of course, if I'm working on this theory, I also need to keep in mind his age at the time of the war. That impacts the likelihood of his enlisting as well. Have you thought about what was going on locally, regionally, nationally, and worldwide at the time of your ancestral problem?

## Is Your Name on Your Flash Drive?

*14 May 2009*

Many of us use flash drives in our genealogy work, particularly as we travel and take pictures, scan documents, share files, etc. Your name may be on your flash drive and it may have a key chain or lanyard with your name on it. Another approach is to have a file in the main directory (preferably a plain text one) with your phone number and email address. That way if the finder is inclined, they have a way to reach you. Of course, backing up your flash drive's files remotely is a good idea as well, but it never hurts to have your bases covered.

## What Have You Ignored?

*16 May 2009*

For a long time, I never really used the International Genealogical Index (IGI) on the *FamilySearch* site (www.familysearch.com) much at all. Most of my ancestors were German, Irish, or Early American, and I just never found anything that I didn't already know and filtering through all the erroneous entries diverted me from more productive pursuits. However, when I started working on my wife's English immigrants, I've had to change my tune. The IGI includes significant extractions from English parish records and they have helped me refine my searches. Keep in mind that the IGI is a derivative source and that in the cases where I was researching, they usually didn't extract deaths. It was mainly births and marriages—at least originally. One should not assume the IGI has every parish. They didn't extract father's occupation and specific residence, which may also be on the original record. The IGI is not an end in and of itself and information it contains should be verified with actual sources as the IGI also contains information from trees and files submitted by church members in the early days of its compilation. Those submissions often had no documentation and can be incorrect. The IGI is a finding aid that can lead to other records and sometimes it is something completely undocumented included in a "family tree." Is there some source you've been in the habit of ignoring that perhaps you should start checking?

## Clues in the Inventory?

*16 May 2009*

Does your ancestor's estate inventory give an idea of his occupation? Many with ancestors who died before the 1850 US census don't have a record that spells out an ancestor's occupation. We may think we have an idea of what they did, but that idea may not be as correct as we think. The record of what was in your ancestor's personal estate might suggest how he earned his living. Keep in mind that there are some items that most households in 1830, 1730, etc. typically had, so be careful drawing conclusions and compare your ancestor's inventory to a few others just to see what items distinguish one from another.

## Updating Your Email?

*17 May 2009*

Have you updated your email address to those old posts you have made to message boards years ago? Is it possible that there are old messages you have sitting out there with your old email attached? While you can't change the old posts, you may be able to post a new message, restating your problem and including your new email. That way someone who finds the old post and your old email address can then search and find your new one. I searched for one of my old email addresses and got over 1,000 hits. Some are for articles I wrote years ago, but a few are on genealogy message boards. Try a Google search for your old email address and see how many times it comes up. Have you posted updates to those boards?

## Are You Really Working the Chain of Migration?

*18 May 2009*

I'm a big believer in chains of migration, but while working on my wife's Frame family I completely ignored the concept. My theory was that since the 1869 era immigrant went to Chicago and was a painter that he simply settled there because he thought he could find work. It seemed like a reasonable premise. When searching for all his family's US census entries, I noted that one child was born in Pennsylvania. I initially wrote it off as a one-time error—an outlier, if you will. When searching UK census records on his in-laws, I noted that his wife had nephews in the UK who indicated they were born in Pennsylvania. Maybe there was a chain of migration after all, and I need to remind myself to look at the in-laws as well!

## Avoid Court Day

*19 May 2009*

If your genealogy travel plans include a trip to that local county courthouse, consider avoiding court offices on "court day" if possible. Some county courts don't meet every day and if you are trying to use records on the one day a week court is in session, you may get less help than usual from the staff. After all, you are an out-of-towner who does not vote or pay local taxes and sometimes that makes a difference in how one is viewed in certain local record offices. Try to find out from the local office if some days are better than others to come in and do research.

*Walter Rampley, Herschel Neill, Cecil Neill, Nellie (Neill) Shanks, [child in front] Lester Rampley, Ralph Neill, Edna (Rampley) Dion*

*probably taken about 1923*

*near West Point, Hancock County, Illinois*

# Chapter 6: Reused Names, Absolute Relationships, Leave the 21St Century

## Get the Real Deal

*20 May 2009*

Remember when requesting copies of vital records to get an actual copy of the document, not just a "proof" or a certification that the event was recorded. Genealogists usually need all the information on the original document in the original handwriting. When I got a copy of my daughter's birth certificate, they brought out a typed copy that basically just gave her name, date and place of birth. While it worked for non-genealogy purposes, I want the "real deal" for my records. My original birth certificate has my mother's signature on it. A transcription won't.

## Check out the County Seat

*21 May 2009*

Before making a trip to that out-of-the-way county courthouse, find out a few things about the county seat:

- Is there someplace to get lunch?
- Should I stay at the local motels?
- Can I use a digital camera?

We were in a very rural county seat several years ago and the town only had a post office. There was no restaurant, no motel, etc. Discover these things before you arrive, not after. Consider posting a query to the appropriate Rootsweb mailing list, Ancestry.com message board (or Facebook group/page) about your trip to find out these things before your arrival. You may also wish to contact the courthouse, library, or local historical/genealogical society for additional details or suggestions.

## Calculated Dates of Birth

*22 May 2009*

If you have a relative's age at death and no stated date of birth, keep in mind that the resulting birthdate (calculated from the age) may be slightly off. First it required the informant to know the exact date of birth and also required them to make the calculation of age correctly. Without knowing the birth date they used to determine the age, there is no way of knowing if stated age is correct. Always put the qualifier "calculated" in front of these dates of birth. This is done to avoid suggesting the document stated the exact date of birth, if it did not. If the person was "older" at the time of their death, the age given at that point in time is secondary information and so is the calculated date of birth.

## State Censuses

*23 May 2009*

Many states took state censuses at some point in their history. Consider expanding your search of census records beyond federal census records. State censuses were often taken in off-census years, frequently in years ending in a "5," but there are exceptions. Determine what state censuses were taken in the locations in which your family lived.

## Wife with the Same Name

*25 May 2009*

There is a tombstone in the local cemetery. I can't remember the husband's name, but he had two wives, both were named Mathilda. One can only imagine how confusing this might be for his descendants and perhaps it was for him during his lifetime as well. Usually a new wife has a different name, but not always. If I researched this individual, the age of his wife might change significantly in census records, her birthplace may suddenly be different, or other pieces of information might seem to be inconsistent. After all, the first name is the same. Keep in mind that if the details on a spouse are different, it might because there was a different spouse—just one with the same first name.

## Did they Reuse Names?

*27 May 2009*

Yesterday's post mentioned men who might have had wives with the same first name. Keep in mind that in some ethnic backgrounds, "reusing" names of deceased children was a very common practice. One of my Ostfriesen ancestral couples had four daughters named Reenste born within a ten-year time span. The first three died shortly after birth. The fourth grew to adulthood. My genealogy software program thought I was nuts to have a family with four children with the same name and I got warning after warning, but it can happen. Men may also name a child after a deceased wife. That's reusing a name in a different sense. While today the practice is not common, there were times and places where it was not considered unusual.

## Are you Backing Up?

*27 May 2009*

One never knows when the hard drive will crash. Are you backing up your genealogy files on a regular basis? Remember, it's not whether your hard drive will fail, but when it will fail.

## How Was Life Different?

*28 May 2009*

Have you really thought about how your ancestor's life was different from your own? Things have changed since your deceased ancestor was alive. Some of those changes are big and some are small. I haven't used directory information to get a phone number for years. Today I simply search for it on my phone. Ten years ago, I couldn't do that. And twenty years ago, it never entered my head to have my phone in my pocket. Maybe when you think about how your ancestor's life is different from your own, you will realize there is something about that ancestor you have overlooked.

## More than Birth and Death Dates

*29 May 2009*

Are you working to get more than just birth and death dates for your ancestors? After a while, lists of names and dates get a little dry for even the most serious genealogist. Consider fleshing out other details on your ancestor. County histories, newspapers, and court records are all great places to get beyond the bare facts. In lectures, I refer to my ancestor's 1850-era Mississippi River tavern as "Barbara's Bar and Grill." The local newspaper referred to it as a "house of ill repute." You never know what you will find until you look. I still don't have Barbara's date and place of birth, but I know a lot about her from court records, newspapers, and other sources. And perhaps when I analyze those pieces of information in more detail there will be a lingering clue there about her origins that I have overlooked.

## Don't Judge, Instead think Why?

*30 May 2009*

Upon occasion, one hears a fellow genealogist being slightly judgmental about a specific ancestor. Instead of getting bogged down in that line of thinking (which doesn't help your research any, to be honest,) think "why?" Putting yourself in your ancestor's shoes gives you a different perspective. If in 1856 you were twenty-six years old, widowed, the mother of two small children, unable to speak English, and living where you had no relatives, what might you do? You might marry the first German speaking single male around—one who would not have been your choice if you were twenty years old and still living at home with no children to support. If your great-grandfather "disappeared," consider where he might have gone and what he might have done. Was there a war he might have enlisted in? Did he have some type of psychological problems? Maybe it was even better that he left, despite the disruption it caused in the family. If you never personally knew the ancestor, leave the judging to someone else. Focus instead on your research. On the flip side of this, I know one researcher who thought it was "romantic" that her great-great-grandmother found the "love of her life" and left her husband and headed out West on some grand adventure. The researcher was completely enamored with the story. Now if *her mother* had done the same thing, I'm certain her response would have been somewhat different.

## Start A Blog

*31 May 2009*

You may think that the world doesn't need any more genealogy blogs, but here's a reason to start one: a relative might contact you. My recent postings about my findings at the Family History Library in Salt Lake brought about a reply from a researcher in Scotland who descends from my wife's 4th great-grandparents. I searched for these ancestors in several online databases, all to no avail. Despite this lack of luck, within two weeks of my posting about the family there was an email in my inbox. I'm not saying you have to blog every day, or even every week. Personally, I'd rather do actual research and analyze what I have, but an occasional entry about what you have found might bring another relative out of the woodwork. There are several sites where users can create blogs with little technical knowledge, including www.blogger.com and www.wordpress.com.

## What's Rare Here is Common There

*01 June 2009*

Keep in mind that a last name that may be unusual in one area may be very common in another. The name Schulmeyer is not too common in Iowa, where my wife's relatives settled in the 1850s. When I looked at the church records for Beberstedt, Germany, however, where the family was from, there were several of them. It seemed when looking at the church christenings that half the births were either to a Schulmeyer mother or a Schulmeyer father. A slight exaggeration, perhaps, but close enough to the truth to keep me on my research toes. Just because a name is rare in your neck of the woods does not mean it is rare in everyone else's.

## Do You Have it at Home?

*02 June 2009*

Keeping track of what you research is important so that you don't spend time looking at the same materials or trying to find something you already have. While at the Family History Library in Salt Lake last month, I had a few spare moments before the library closed. I decided to copy references from a Mercer County, Kentucky, marriage book. I was so proud of myself for finding something to do at the last minute and getting "something done." Problem was, I already had the actual book at home. I did not need copies of pages from it. So much for "dreaming" up what to do when my to do list runs short.

## Relationships Are Not Always Absolute

*03 June 2009*

Just because someone is listed as someone's child in a census enumeration doesn't mean they actually were their biological child. It is not unusual for a stepchild to be referred to as someone's child in a census enumeration, although many census enumerators did make the distinction. Pre-1880 census records in the United States do not even list the relationship to head of household, creating additional confusion. Could a child have been a stepchild or a neighbor child who was taken in? And if person A is person B's "cousin," the exact biological relationship may not be as simple as one thinks. Their parents could have been siblings or half-siblings or the relationship could have been even more distant. And even though relationships were to be to the head of the household, that doesn't mean that errors don't slip in.

## A License Doesn't Mean They Got Married

*06 June 2009*

Just because your ancestor took out a marriage license does not necessarily mean they got married. Make certain there is a return of the license to the clerk or records office. That document should have the date of the ceremony provided by the officiant. Most people who take out a license actually get married, but once in a while something happens between the courthouse and the ceremony. Sometimes that "something" happens after the marriage and a divorce record is the result.

## Naming Patterns are Not Absolute

*08 June 2009*

In some families and ethnic groups, there are tendencies to pass on certain names in certain ways. There can be variations on this theme and many ethnic groups claim that the pattern is always practiced by them or belongs exclusively to them. While a practice may be common, there is no guarantee that it always happens. Perhaps the oldest son is named for the father's father, the oldest daughter for the father's mother, and then on down the line. Remember that this practice was a tendency in some families and is not proof of anyone's name at all. Names of potential parents based on naming patterns can be used as clues, but they are "extremely circumstantial" ones at best. Just because a couple named their first son Henry does not *necessarily mean that the paternal grandfather **has** to be a Henry.* And if both grandfathers are named John and both grandmothers are named Anna, then you really have a mess...naming pattern or not! These patterns are clues and clues are not the same as facts.

## Learn About a New Record

*11 June 2009*

Is there some record type of source you have never utilized because you thought it was too difficult to use, too difficult to understand, or too hard to access? Consider expanding your research horizons and make today (or this week) the time you use that new (to you) source. You may make some wonderful discoveries. Limiting yourself to certain records when others are available limits the information you could discover.

## Filename Make Sense?

*12 June 2009*

I wasted an hour today looking for a set of documents I scanned a year or so ago. I scanned and saved them when I was in a hurry and the file name was not very helpful: "ufkes." There was nothing more to it than that. When a last name of a file is the same as your mother's maiden name (which it is in this case), many genealogy files contain that word. I eventually searched the entire hard drive for files with "ufkes" in the title, but there were many that I had to go through. I renamed the file with a more descriptive name: "john_ufkes_cancelled_homestead_file."

It is also good advice to organize scanned images the moment you save them and not wait until later. Had my file been in the folder of materials I already have for this ancestor, (which uses his name and his year of birth) it would have been much easier to locate.

Are your file names helpful? Are your files organized at least by person in a way that helps you find them? And do you file them as you make them?

## Research the Families You "Know"

*13 June 2009*

Researching more "completely" a family you think you already know everything about may do one of several things for you or for your research. You may learn something about research or something about the family you did not know before. Those are skills that can be used on families where your knowledge is more lacking. Recently, I obtained deeds showing how a house and a farm were sold after the owners died. In both cases, I knew all the vital event dates and relationships within the family. In both cases, I understood and interpreted the records better because I "knew" the family. That helps me understand records later when I don't know the family as well or many details about them. Sometimes it is easier to learn about records when the family isn't as foreign to you as the records. And in one case I even learned a few things about the family that were new to me. Another reason to search for everything.

## Could It Be Years After?

*14 June 2009*

Have you thought about how long after your ancestor's death he or she may be mentioned in a record? My ancestor Peter Bieger died in Illinois in 1855. He is mentioned by name in a 1906 deed when his grandchildren signed a quitclaim deed for the property to clean up issues to the title. That was fifty-one years after he died.

## Before You Buy that CD on eBay

*19 June 2009*

A little piece of advice: before you buy a CD with a PDF or a scan of that out of print book on eBay (or anywhere else), make certain a digital copy of that book is not available for free on one of the many websites that has complete digital images of out-of-print materials such as *GoogleBooks* (books.google.com) or www.archive.org.

## Do You Really Know It?

*20 June 2009*

How many pieces of information are in your family tree or genealogy database because they came from your "memory" or some unidentified source? Check them out and, if something is from your memory and there are no other records of it elsewhere, indicate you are the source. The other pieces of information for which you have no reference may be correct—or they may be incorrect. And the incorrect ones could be the reason for your struggles in locating more information.

## Actually Transcribe Something

*21 June 2009*

Scanning documents or making digital images by taking pictures of them is an excellent way to share and preserve them, but there's more you can and should do. Transcribing documents serves a purpose: it forces you to actually *read* the document. That is a great way to notice phrases or words that sometimes get overlooked. And there are times when that one word or phrase can make all the difference. Transcriptions can also be searched for specific words or phrases. Transcribe something today.

## Go Back and Revisit

*23 June 2009*

Periodically revisit sites that contain data you have used in your family history research. It is not necessary to revisit them every day, but monthly or even quarterly visits may result in undiscovered finds. No matter how much you think you keep up to date on genealogical "news," something can easily slip past your radar. New information is always being made available, many times without a PR firm or blogger broadcasting it to the world. Take the time to look. Make a list of sites and visit them regularly. Not obsessively, however!

## Why Did They Move?

*24 June 2009*

There are several factors that might have caused your ancestor to move from point A to point B. They include:

- Economic concerns—land opportunities, jobs, etc.
- Politics and political unrest
- Family—others in their family had already moved.
- Acquaintances/friends—people in this group had already moved.
- Religion—your ancestor was a part of a religious group that migrated.

There are other reasons but consider these and ask yourself if you have really looked into these causes and how much you are aware of these events in your relative's life. Doing so may provide the answer to your family history puzzle.

## Name Changes in Probate Records

*25 June 2009*

Read through all those papers in a probate file or an estate settlement. The widow may be listed under a new married name in later records in the file, providing a clue to a subsequent marriage. This can be a great help in states that do not have marriage records for the time period being researched.

## Get Out of the 21st Century

*27 June 2009*

Remember that we do not live in the same time as our ancestors—at least for the most part, depending upon your age. If you are working on families from two hundred years ago, consider reading contemporary material from that era. Transcribed diaries, newspapers, and other materials are a great way to get a better "feel" for the times, in addition to reading non-fiction history covering the same time period. Reading someone else's diary from the time, even if a complete non-relative, may give you a fresh perspective on your ancestor's life and times. Remember that most TV shows and other types of drama don't always present a realistic view of life in the past.

## Get Out of that Rut

*28 June 2009*

Are you checking the same sites almost too regularly, hoping for an update? Are you posting queries to message boards and other sites, hoping to find something or get a helpful reply? Consider changing your approach or spending less time on the Internet or more time on different sites. My *Ancestry.com* subscription lapsed recently and I decided to wait to renew it. My research has not stopped or suffered. Now that I don't have 24/7 access to it, I am getting back into records I had ignored for too long and am even reviewing my files. I'm focusing on records that are offline and not available digitally. And when I do re-activate my access to Ancestry. com (which I eventually will), I will hopefully make better use of it. And frankly some days I spent too much time "randomly" searching on *Ancestry.com* and not enough time really researching.

## It Goes Both Ways

*30 June 2009*

If you know the name of the church, if the records are extant, and if the church practiced infant baptism, it is relatively easy to find the names of those who were godparents for your ancestor's children. Those names are clues as they are potential relatives. However, when the records are unindexed, finding the names of children for whom your ancestor was a godparent is not as easy. It requires manual searching of each baptismal entry, but may be worth it, because the parents of that child for whom your ancestor was a godparent are just as big a clue as who the godparents were of your ancestor's children. That relationship cuts both ways. Don't search just one side of that equation.

## Census Search Trick

*01 July 2009*

If you can't find your ancestor in the 1840 census and you think he really should be there, look for his 1830 neighbors in 1840 or try looking for his 1850 neighbors in 1840. No guarantees, but it's worth a shot.

*Fred Ufkes (1893-1960)*

*About 1910*

*Basco, Hancock County, Illinois*

# Chapter 7: Nicknames, Endogamy, Census Bridges, and Vacuums

## Stop and Organize

*03 July 2009*

I've been working on my wife's English lines lately. Some have been fairly easy to research and I have been accumulating quite a bit of information, digital copies of records, etc. There comes a time when one must stop and really put together and organize what one has. I have many copies and notes, but I have not put the information into my database where I can see what families I have information on, where I have gaps, etc. The names and the families are all starting to run together. The research is fun, but every so often you need to stop gathering and start organizing, if for no other reason than to not completely confuse yourself.

## Check Before and After

*04 July 2009*

If you find an ancestor's deed in a land record book, check the pages before and after the document you located. It was not uncommon for individuals to record certain documents in "groups" (land records are probably the best example of this) and more than one record may have been filed at the same time.

## Should You Ever Use a Nickname as Your Ancestor's Given Name in Your Database?

*05 July 2009*

Purists would say you should use whatever is on a birth certificate as an individual's given name in your genealogy database. After all, that's often their "legal name." I think some discretion should be used when choosing the name that you use to refer to your ancestor. My great-grandmother's birth certificate lists her name as Frances Iona Rampley. However, every document she actually signed from her marriage document through records settling her husband's estate lists her as Fannie Neill (her married name). Her tombstone even has her listed as Fannie Neill. While I can't be certain who decided how her name was to be put on her stone, it was very likely her or her children. Interestingly enough, she would occasionally use her middle initial but not her middle name. In my database her name is listed as Fannie as apparently that is what she wanted to be called. That's the name I use for her when writing about her. In my notes, there is information about her birth certificate and the name it actually lists, and my transcription of the birth certificate includes the name as given.

## Are You Only Using One Source for Every Event?

*07 July 2009*

Different records for the same event may provide different information about that event. While it is not always possible to "doublecheck" everything, try to obtain multiple sources of information for events whenever you can. One record can easily be incorrect.

## The Importance of Endogamy

*08 July 2009*

Genealogists may not be familiar with the word, but they should be familiar with the concept. Endogamy is the practice of marrying within the social group. Greek immigrants to Chicago tend to marry other Greek immigrants (or children of Greek immigrants). Missouri settlers from Tennessee tend to have children who marry into other nearby families of settlers from Tennessee. While individuals can easily marry "outside" the group, a shared heritage (be it from across the "big pond" or across the creek) can be a big factor in the eventual choice of a marriage partner. It explains why half my own ancestors are Ostfriesen even though my families had all lived in the United States for nearly 100 years before I was born.

## Why Does Immigrant Great-great-grandma Have No Naturalization?

*10 July 2009*

Before 1922, most US women derived citizenship from their husband or their father. Before women had the right to vote, citizenship was not as critical as one may think since voting is one of the key rights only allowed to citizens. Women in many states could own property whether or not they were a citizen. One exception was that women who wanted to file a homestead claim in their own name needed to be a citizen. As a result, single female immigrants who wanted to acquire a federal homestead would need to naturalize. Other than that, few women before 1922 bothered to naturalize in the United States.

## Does Paying Property Taxes Mean Grandpa Lived There?

*11 July 2009*

Keep in mind that paying property tax only indicates an individual owned property in a specific location. It does not mean that he necessarily lived there, although many property owners lived relatively close to their owned property. While there are always exceptions, you shouldn't use property tax payment as evidence of residence. Paying a personal property tax is different as it usually indicates residence in the area in which the tax was paid.

## Do You Know When Civil Registration Starts in Your Areas of Research?

*12 July 2009*

If you do not know when civil registration starts in the jurisdictions in which you are researching, find out. And if you don't know what civil registration is, then there's even more work for you to do. It's governmental recording of vital events—births and deaths. While marriages are typically considered a vital record, they are slightly different as they are a contract between two individuals. Births and deaths are not contracts.

## Behaving at the Research Facility?

*13 July 2009*

Remember when at the library, there are others present beside you. Be considerate of them. I'm fairly patient, but here are a few things that have given me cause for frustration lately:

- A gentleman having a cell phone conversation in the library about going fishing. He was yelling into his phone. It was all I could do to concentrate. Hopefully he doesn't yell when he goes fishing.
- Two researchers lamenting the destruction of tombstones in an Alabama town. While I understood the frustration, a twenty-minute diatribe about the injustice of it all was highly distracting and did not need to take place in the library.

Be considerate of your fellow researchers. You may one day be at the library trying to read illegible script when someone sitting next to you is carrying on very loudly about the latest injustice their son-in-law has inflicted on their daughter. While he may be a lout, the discussion can be had elsewhere.

## Learn How to Communicate Silently

*13 July 2009*

When one travels a great distance to research onsite in actual records repositories, it is important to make the best use of your time. I do not want to be running to another area of the facility or go outside to have phone conversations. Instead of using the cellphone for the occasional "emergency" back home, my family, other researchers, and I communicate via text or a messaging app instead.

## Know the Terrain

*14 July 2009*

Learn about the geography of where your ancestor lived. It might explain where they later settled, how they travelled, where they went to church, got married, etc. The easiest place to get to because of geographic constraints may have been in an adjoining county or further, "as the crow flies."

## Get a Research Plan

*15 July 2009*

Don't just research mindlessly. It is bad in more ways than one. Decide what you want to know, determine what you already know, and learn about ways to get there. Research plans need to be more detailed than this, obviously, but don't do your research in a haphazard fashion.

## If You Can't Go Up, Go Down

*16 July 2009*

If you have gotten stuck in extending your family back to earlier generations, consider tracking the descendants of that earliest "unknown" ancestor. Perhaps one of his other descendants has information, sources, or family mementos of which you are unaware. Tracking those descendants will also prove helpful in analyzing your DNA test results.

## What Makes a Source Citation?

*17 July 2009*

I'm not going to summarize Elizabeth Shown Mills' *Evidence Explained* in one tip but, generally speaking, a source citation should provide enough information to allow you or someone else to get back to the actual record you used to cite a date or an event in the same format that you accessed it (original, digital, microfilm, etc.). That citation should also include information in regards to the provenance of the source, its perceived reliability, and whether it is an original or some type of derivation from the original.

## Get Every Census

*18 July 2009*

Do you have your ancestor in every extant census in which she would be enumerated? Skipping one because "it won't tell you anything" is never a good idea. One never knows what surprising information may be lurking in a "routine" census enumeration.

## Census Should Be a Bridge to Something Else

*19 July 2009*

For every census listing you have for an ancestor, think of other sources and materials suggested by that enumeration. A value of real property in an 1860 census indicates land and property tax records. A personal property valuation in an 1850 census suggests personal property tax records. An occupation may suggest local county records or occupational records, and children with different last names in the household suggest multiple marriages or extended family who may have been living in the household, at least temporarily.

## You Can Still Go Page-By-Page

*20 July 2009*

Back in the "old days" of genealogy research, searching page-by-page was often the only way to find someone in a census record. With the advent of every name indexes, "point and click" research is how many people search and access census records. There are times when it does not work, and there are times where if you know where your ancestor lived, that "traditional" approaches may be faster. A careful page-by-page reading of the census in the area where your ancestor lived may tell you more than you'll learn just by reading your ancestor's entry.

## Laws Change Over Time

*21 July 2009*

We all know that laws change. We just sometimes forget that those changes may apply to our genealogy. Early in my research, I was surprised to learn that when my uncle died in 1907, without any children, his wife did not automatically inherit his entire estate. She inherited a part of it as his wife, but the balance went to his heirs. In this case, his siblings and some of his nieces and nephews (children of a deceased brother) were also heirs to his estate. Imagine sharing your deceased spouse's estate with your in-laws. It made for an interesting court case when the wife's portion of the real estate could be not be equitably partitioned out to her.

## Get Out of Your Vacuum

*22 July 2009*

Are you in isolation in your research? If there are not relatives (close or distant) working on your same family lines, consider joining a mailing list at Rootsweb (lists.rootsweb.com), a genealogical Facebook group, etc. There are lists and groups that are global or national in their scope, but there are other regional lists devoted to smaller regions including ethnic areas, states, counties, former countries, etc. Even if you don't find a relative in one of these groups, someone working in the same location as you can be an excellent resource.

## Get Religion?

*23 July 2009*

If your ancestors were members of a denomination for a significant length of time, learn something of that denomination's history. A broad understanding of their religion may provide you with insight into their life, what might have motivated your relative to do what they did (or move where they did), and why the church kept the type of records it did.

## Sort the Tradition

*24 July 2009*

Family traditions can run the gamut. They can range from comical to depressing and from reasonable to completely outrageous. Wherever they fit on the scale, they are often not 100% correct. Few things are actually completely and totally correct. What I like to do with family traditions is to sort the details they contain into facts that might have generated records and facts that probably did not generate records. I keep in mind that "facts" stated in a family tradition may or may not be true. That's why we research them.

## Early Conclusions?

*26 July 2009*

When was the last time you reviewed records and conclusions made early in your research? Is it possible that mistakes made early in your research are giving you problems today?

## Checked all Jurisdictions

*27 July 2009*

Have you checked for potential records at the town or village, township, county, state and federal level? Focusing on just one level of records may cause you to miss vital sources. This is true for the United States and Europe as well. The names of the jurisdictions may be different, but remember that any one physical location may be a contained in several different levels of government. Each of those levels may have generated their own records.

# It Will Conflict

*28 July 2009*

Sooner or later you will encounter conflicting information in your research. Record the information as it is provided on each source and put any analysis in your notes—clearly separate from your transcription of the document. Do not change, correct, or modify the information from an actual record. Your job is not to edit. If there are obvious errors, indicate that in a comment, but do not "fix" the record.

# Why Do Early US Naturalization Records Contain Little Information?

*29 July 2009*

Because US law did not require it. In 1906 there was reform of immigration and the naturalization process in the United States. This reform resulted in more paperwork, fewer courts being allowed to naturalize citizens, and more detail in the records. Consequently, the records after that reform provide more information on the applicant. If your ancestors naturalized shortly before 1906, determine if there were relatives who might have naturalized after the reform that might have left more detailed records.

# Do You Have the Correct Location?

*30 July 2009*

Is it possible that the town name of the location is right, but the name of the state is incorrect? Is it possible that part of the name is right, but the remaining portion has been spelled or pronounced incorrectly? Did your ancestor give the name of the closest "big town" instead of saying where he was actually from?

## Problem-Solving in a Nutshell

*31 July 2009*

If you are stuck, you should decide what the problem is, what the sources are, how those sources are organized, and how those sources are searched. Search those records, track your search, and evaluate the results. That's a broad overview, but this process will get you started. Don't forget to learn about your ancestor's social group and about the history of the area where he lived.

## Learn from the Inventory

*01 August 2009*

If you have an estate inventory for your ancestor, have you made an attempt to learn what every item is? Doing so may teach you more about your ancestor's life and potentially even give you a clue as to his occupation.

## Print One Page

*02 August 2009*

Before going to a library to research, print out one page that contains a bibliographic citation for each source or reference you wish to use while there. Then you can either take research notes on that page or attach that page to research notes or copies. This effectively serves as an "in the field" research log that can be written up more formally upon returning home. Another approach is to put all the bibliographic information in word processing document along with what families and names you want to look for in each reference. That document can be used for notetaking at the research facility as well—either taking notes on a printed version of document or typing on an electronic version.

# Chapter 8: Popularity, Wrong Grandmas, New Wife

## Are you Sharing or Preserving?

*03 August 2009*

Have you thought about how your information will be shared with others after you leave this Earth? How will your information be preserved? Think about this today rather than putting it off. Tomorrow may be too late. Remember that few relatives, libraries, or archives are going to want an unorganized box of papers, and digital media with thousands of randomly named files aren't too much better—although they do take up less physical space.

## The Unindexed Nature of Court Records

*05 August 2009*

Until they are all digitized and indexed (which is years away from happening, if ever), court records are one of the richest bodies of records that are difficult to access. A court case may contain the names of numerous individuals, and yet is only indexed twice— once under the name of the first plaintiff and once under the name of the first defendant. Because of this, it is imperative to search court indexes for all family members and read those cases that may involve an uncle or aunt or other close family member (particularly if it looks like the case is some sort of family squabble). There is a chance that something is in there about your ancestor as well.

## Was It Just Popular and Has Nothing to do with Family?

*05 August 2009*

My grandmother Neill had a brother named Cecil. Her sister's husband was named Cecil and her own husband (my grandfather) was named Cecil. While I don't know about the brother-in-law's family, I do know that the name of Cecil had not previously appeared in either my grandmother or grandfather's family before the arrival of those two individuals. Apparently at the time of these births, between 1900 and 1915, the name was fairly popular. It wasn't all that popular fifty years earlier and, fifty years later, its popularity was waning. There may be a reason a name "appears out of thin air" in one of your families. Just remember that the name may have no genealogical connection to any other family member. It just might have been in fashion.

## Double Listed in the Census

While reviewing some research done years ago on my Grandmother Neill, I remembered something: anyone can easily be listed twice in the census. They don't have to be a rich and famous world traveler or a migrant moving between locations. My Grandma is listed twice in 1930 in the same area—once with her parents, and once in the household where she was "working out." She is not the only one. Her married brother is listed twice as well. Once with his wife in the town where he grew up, and once in the town 30 miles away where he and his wife had moved for his job around the time of the census. It never hurts to look more than once. And if you think "working out" means exercise, well...it doesn't.

## Multiple Guardians

*08 August 2009*

Keep in mind that a minor could have had several guardians in their life if one of more of their parents were deceased. There are several types of guardians:

- Guardian of the person—responsible for the physical safety and care of the child and the one who had physical custody. Generally speaking, this is the surviving parent.
- Guardian of the estate—watched over the child's inheritance and was legally responsible for the child's

financial interests. This person could be related to the child in some way, but not necessarily.

- *Guardian ad litem*—a guardian appointed who was usually a lawyer to represent a child who was somehow involved in court action.

A *guardian ad litem* was actually serving as the child's "lawyer" and was not a guardian of the child's person or estate. The first two could be the same person, but the guardian of the estate would have to be appointed by the court. Much depends upon the situation.

## Take A Day Off (or Two!)

*09 August 2009*

Are you working on the same family day after day after day? Consider taking a few days off and avoid making genealogy "your job." Coming back later with a fresh perspective might be just what you need to get going again.

## Does the Signature Match the Document?

*10 August 2009*

Does that ancestral signature on a document match the handwriting on the document itself? Don't conclude your ancestor wrote the record. Most likely what you are looking at is a transcription of the record made by the clerk. The clerk likely copied your ancestor's signature as well. All of this was done in the handwriting of the clerk. Always try to determine the original source of the image you have found on the internet or that someone has shared with you. It always helps to know what you are looking at.

## Don't Assume Grandma Was Wrong

*11 August 2009*

My grandma Neill told me she remembered her baptism. I was skeptical as the denomination of which her parents were members practiced infant baptism. Grandma had to be wrong. She was apparently confused. Actually, she was correct. For reasons that are not clear, Grandma was baptized at the age of five along with several of her siblings. She was right. I'll think twice before assuming (without evidence) that someone was wrong.

## Is It Really a Name Change?

*13 August 2009*

A poster to a list indicated that her European ancestor's first name was changed from Andreas to Andrew when he immigrated to the United States. Two things come to mind. His name really wasn't "changed." It was translated in this case. Andreas is Latin and Andrew is English. The second is that if his name changed, it likely was when he naturalized or when he established himself in the area where he settled, not when he landed. Changings at landings were rare—your paperwork when you landed had to match or there could be issues, especially in the mid-19th century and after.

## Got Them All From the SSDI?

*17 August 2009*

Have you searched for every appropriate person in the Social Security Death Index (SSDI)? Are there people in your database who might be in there and for whom you have not searched? It might be worth your while to check it out. The Social Security Death Index is online and free at *FamilySearch* and is also a part of several fee-based database sites. If you do not know who typically is in the SSDI, read the description of the database. It is not an index of every dead person in the United States.

## Did They Move Back and Forth?

*19 August 2009*

Keep in mind that your ancestor may have moved back and forth or all over. Not everyone followed a general path in just one direction. I'm working on a person now who was in Iowa in 1856, Missouri in 1860, Iowa in 1870-1895, Missouri in 1900, Wyoming in 1910 and in Missouri in 1912. Oh, and she was born in either New York State or Canada. Constant movers can be a constant genealogical problem.

## The Census We Use Is Not the Original

*20 August 2009*

Remember that the US census we use today was not the one on which the census taker took his "original" enumeration. The census copy that was microfilmed, and eventually digitized, was the "clean" copy that was written by the census taker after he finished taking the census. He used his field notes to make the good copy that we use today. Any chance there was something in his field notes he couldn't read? And what was the chance that he went back and asked for clarification on an age or place of birth that he could not read? What was the chance that he just guessed if he could not tell if the original age was 18 or 15 on his notes?

## 1925 Iowa State Census?

*21 August 2009*

For those who did not know, the 1925 Iowa State Census asked for names of father and mother of everyone enumerated. The index and images are online at *FamilySearch.* It might be worth a try if you had extended family in Iowa in 1925. They asked where the parents were married, too!

## Don't Rush

*22 August 2009*

I wanted to locate the children of a relative in census records after her death. The names were somewhat common and I didn't have too many details about them. I may wish to try another approach. Maybe I had better wait until I get the obituaries and estate records of the parents. Those documents may provide me with enough clues to find the children in census records and make certain I have the correct ones.

## Widow for a Day or Longer?

*23 August 2009*

I almost overlooked the death certificate of the husband of a female relative. The lady I was researching died in 1914 and was listed as a widow at the time of her death. I didn't look at the death certificate for a man with the same last name who also died in 1914, thinking it could not be her husband. Turns out it was. They died four days apart. Don't assume anything. Being listed as a widow only means her husband died before her. It could have been two days or twenty years.

## Track the Wrong Ones

*24 August 2009*

Keep track of the individuals that you have eliminated as being your ancestor, his parents, his brother, his sister, etc. That way you do not research them again. Include what sources you located on this wrong person and why you think they are not the actual person of interest. That way you have the information if it turns out your initial conclusion was wrong and you need to revisit those records.

## Google Those Wrong Names

*27 August 2009*

A death certificate for a potential relative indicated he died in "tumway, Iowa." I had no idea where that was. I didn't try the United States Geological Survey Geographic Names Information Site, but it wouldn't have made any difference anyway. Googling "tumway iowa" told me that it wasn't probably "tumway" at all. A search for "tumway iowa" resulted in references to Ottumwa, Iowa. I should have thought of that. If the gazetteers don't bring the desired results, try Google and remember that any information provided on a document often comes via the informant's mouth—accent and all.

## Non-Genealogy Databases in Your Local Library

*28 August 2009*

Does your local library have access to databases not specifically genealogy-related that might help you in your research? Libraries may have academic subscriptions to databases for public use onsite (or remote access for cardholders), and those sources may include digitized newspapers, fire insurance maps, and other items of direct genealogical interest. Academic journal articles (particularly in history, culture, and sociology) may contain excellent background reading material on your area of ethnic group of interest. You may be surprised to find that a graduate student published an article on Welsh immigrants to the area in Illinois where your family settled. Ask your local librarian what databases they subscribe to, and do the same for nearby university libraries. Their webpages may indicate what databases and journals for which they provide onsite access. You may have access to more information than you think.

## Do You Have Contemporary Maps of Every Location?

*29 August 2009*

Do you have maps of all your ancestral locations at a time contemporary to your ancestors? It might not be possible to get maps for every ancestor and location you have, but review what maps you have and ask yourself, "is it possible there are more maps" or "is not having a map hindering my research?"

## Getting it All?

*30 August 2009*

Make certain you are getting the entire record. I was recently using marriage records for Champaign County, Illinois. They were on microfilm at the Champaign County Archives in the Urbana Free Library. For the time period I was looking for there were actually two series of marriage records. One was the marriage applications and the other was the actual licenses. If I had been in too much of a hurry, I might have easily overlooked one of the records as they were not filed in the same way I had used them in other locations.

## Don't Be Afraid to Ask Questions

*31 August 2009*

I will admit it. After 25 years of research, occasionally threading a microfilm machine will confuse me. Sometimes I hesitate to ask for help. After all, I should know how to use one, but then I remember waiting only wastes time. If there is something at a library or archives that confuses you or you do not understand, ask. Staff can usually help you operate the equipment but not if you get mad at it first and break it. They may be able to help you with a record or document, give you a reference to read that may be helpful, or indicate someone they know who may be better equipped to give you direction.

# Grandma Gave the Wrong Date Because She Thought it was Right

*02 September 2009*

Did Grandma give the "wrong" date or place of birth for herself? Did she possibly do it because she actually thought that is where or when she was born? Keep in mind that on many records where our ancestors provided information on themselves that they were not actually asked for any sort of documentation. The clerk just wrote down what the informant provided. My own Grandma, who would have been 99 today, always gave the same place as her place of birth. Problem is, her birth certificate and other contemporary records give a different location. Grandma just had a misconception about where she was born based on where her father had grown up and where her parents originally lived. Sometimes errors are actually mistakes, not intentional lies.

# They Weren't Asked How to Spell It

*03 September 2009*

When I got married, one of the questions on the license was mother's maiden name. I knew I was going to have to spell it. After all, I wasn't getting married in the small town that I grew up where the last name was well-known. I had to spell it three times before he understood, and it was only five letters—Ufkes. Chances are your ancestor was not asked to spell the information he provided on a record. And if you think he did spell it to the clerk, how can you really be certain that's what happened? After all, you weren't there when the clerk asked great-great-grandfather for the information on his marriage. And if you were there—there were a lot of questions that I bet you wish you had asked!

## Did they Change Churches?

*04 September 2009*

My maternal ancestors have been members of the same denomination since the Reformation. I was floored when I read the obituary for two of my great-great-grandparents and it said the funeral was at the local Presbyterian church. There was a reason: the small town only had two churches. Neither was of the desired denominations was the "right" one. The Presbyterian church was closest. Is it possible that necessity caused your ancestor to attend (and leave records at) a church other than the one you think he always attended?

## Disbanded Churches?

*05 September 2009*

If your ancestor's church disbanded, there are several places the records might have gone:

- the local dump
- the family of the last minister
- a local church of the same denomination
- a regional or national church organization, synod, assembly, diocese, etc.

Contact local historical or genealogical societies, local churches of the same denomination, and regional and national archives (or governing bodies) of the denomination to see if they know what might have happened to the records.

## Things Get Filed Incorrectly

*07 September 2009*

Keep in mind that records do get misfiled as clerks are human. Packets of court papers do not get put back in the correct numerical order. Case numbers get written incorrectly in indexes. Page numbers get transcribed incorrectly as they are typed or entered into an index. Errors will happen. Think about how something could have gotten misfiled when you cannot find it in the place where it is "supposed" to be. Could digits have been transposed? Could a "6" have been read as a "0," etc.?

## Did Great Grandma Really Say That?

*07 September 2009*

On my great-grandmother's 1935 marriage application, her place of birth is given. The problem is that it is significantly different from places listed for her on other records. It's also clearly wrong based on what I know about her parent's lives at the time of her birth. Why did she list that location? I'm not certain why and I'm not even certain she actually gave the information. Remember, her husband was also there when the license was taken out, and it is possible that he gave information on his wife. It's also possible she got mixed up or intentionally lied. I wasn't there when great-grandma got married to witness the giving of the information, so I don't *know* who gave it. The form doesn't really say who provided what. Keep that in mind.

## Write Down Everything

*08 September 2009*

You will forget. You will not remember it. And you will wonder where you put it or where you found it. Write it down. Do not use little pieces of paper. They get lost and you will lose your mind looking for them.

## Help Someone You Aren't Related To

*09 September 2009*

Has someone posted a question you can answer to an email list or to Facebook page or group? Has someone requested pictures at a cemetery near where you live? Give back just a little and help someone else out. You never know when you may need help, and sometimes when thinking about someone else's problem, you have an idea about your own. That may be a selfish reason to help, but sometimes it really happens.

## Learn About Your Ancestor's Occupation

*10 September 2009*

What do you really know about your ancestor's occupation and how he or she probably lived their life? Learning about the tools of their trade or what life was like for the typical cotton warper, mill worker, tailor, etc. may give you some additional insight into your ancestor's life. Even if you think you know, you might not. I grew up on a farm, but farm life when I grew up was different from when my father did (we never had horses for one), and it was certainly different from when my great-great-grandparents were farming. The first time I read of a "stationary baler" in a pension file, I did not know what it was. Hay balers, as far as I was concerned, were never stationary and were pulled behind a tractor. Then it dawned on me that, in 1900, they would have taken the hay to the baler. Hence the term, stationary baler. If you read the term "stationary baler" as an item in a 1900 era probate file, would you even have known what it was? Sometimes Google helps with these things and sometimes it doesn't.

## Does the Answer to the Past Lie in the Present?

*11 September 2009*

My wife's great-grandfather William Frame Apgar was born as William Frame in Chicago, Illinois, around 1888. Around 1918, he disappeared, estranged from his wife—my wife's great-grandmother. Perhaps he enlisted in the war, perhaps not. None of my wife's immediate family knows what happened to him. It is possible that his siblings might have known what happened to him and passed that information down. My answer to where William Frame Apgar went might rest in the descendants of his siblings and not in the descendants of his children.

# Naming Patterns and What Your Ancestor Has to Do

*12 September 2009*

The first son was named for this, the second son was named for that, etc. Keep in mind that these patterns are trends and social customs that your ancestor might have followed. They are not law. Your ancestor does not have to follow any of these "social mores." What your ancestor does have to do is:

- Figure out how to get born
- Figure out how to get married (or at least reproduce)
- Leave behind at least one record

Dying usually happens whether your ancestor planned for it or not.

# Now Wife

*13 September 2009*

If your ancestor uses the phrase "now wife" in his will, it does not mean that he was married before. It was used to make the intent of a legal document clear. If Johann gives his farm to "my now wife and after her death to my children," it means his wife at the time the will was written. This was done to see to it that if the wife the testator was married to at the time his will was written died and the testator remarried, that the children and not the current wife inherited the property. Without the word "now," "wife" is potentially vague. The phrase "now wife" was used to clear things up, but it has confused many genealogists.

# Were They Really from the Same Village?

*14 September 2009*

My wife and I both have a set of ancestors who were immigrants and I think the groom wrote back and said, "I need a bride." One might be tempted to think that the bride and groom were born in the same village just because they were from the same village. That's not necessarily true. The father of one bride was a migrating "windmill mechanic" who eventually moved his family to the village where the groom was from. The other bride was working as a hired girl in the village where the groom was born and raised. Sometimes romantic visions of our ancestors need to be discarded. Good fiction is not always good genealogy and sometimes reality is more interesting.

## State versus Federal Land States

*15 September 2009*

State land states are those states where the original "seller" on the first deed transferring real property to private ownership was the state—actually the colony. State land states are generally the thirteen original colonies, states that bordered them, and a few others. Federal land states are those where the original "seller" on the first deed transferring ownership to a private citizen was the federal government. Usually these states are areas settled after the Northwest Ordinance of 1787. State land states usually describe their land in metes and bounds. Federal land states usually use base lines and meridians in legal descriptions, but there are exceptions.

## The Names the Same

*17 September 2009*

Just to confuse genealogists, some states have towns that are not located in the county with the same name. Des Moines, Iowa, is not located in Des Moines County, Iowa. Keokuk, Iowa, is not located in Keokuk County, Iowa. It's not just an Iowa thing. This can happen anywhere. Make certain your place descriptions are complete and not misleading. I always use the word "county" just to keep things clear.

# Is it Time to Hire Someone?

*18 September 2009*

I recently needed eight land entry files from the National Archives. I knew some of these files would not contain very much information at all, perhaps just a few sheets. There were three that had the potential to contain valuable information as they were homestead and preemption claims. To order the files directly from the National Archives would have cost me over three hundred dollars. I hired a researcher to go to the Archives and copy the files for me. The fee was approximately one-fourth what I would have paid the archives. Is it possible that hiring someone at the remote record site is the way to go?

# Not Digital, not Filmed, not Transcribed

*18 September 2009*

When was the last time you accessed a record that was not on microfilm, not in digital form, not published, and not indexed? Remember that there are millions of documents in courthouses, archives, etc. that only exist on paper. Is the answer to your question written on a piece of paper that you or someone else will have to actually see in person to get a copy? Not everything is on film or available digitally.

# *Evidence Explained*: Not Just About Citations

*20 September 2009*

*Evidence Explained* by Elizabeth Shown Mills is not just about citing sources. The first two chapters are wonderful genealogical lessons on methodology and the essentials of citation. Before discussing how to cite a specific type of record, Mills briefly discusses that record, providing an overview. While Mills' book is not for the new genealogist, this not-so-new genealogist finds its discussion of sources an excellent quick review and primer when I need reminding.

## Not Everything has Page Numbers

*21 September 2009*

Old documents and genealogical records usually have pages (except for tombstones and photographs), but they might not have page numbers. Church records are especially notorious for this, especially in the days when records were kept in blank ledgers without printed forms. To keep track of where you got an image of a church record or some other record in an unpaginated book, at least indicate the year of the record and what type of record it was (christenings, funerals, marriages, etc.). The name of the church and its location should also be included as a part of your source citation, but the year and type of record are essential to know where you got the information. If the entries are numbered for each year, include the entry number as well.

## Is it Alphabetical?

*23 September 2009*

Look at that census or tax list again. Do the names on the page for your ancestor all begin with the same letter? If so, the collector or census taker tried to sort the names alphabetically. Good for him. Bad for us as it strips all sense of neighborhood. People do not live in alphabetical order.

## Look at All Those Page Numbers

*23 September 2009*

When downloading a census page or viewing a census on microfilm, look at all the page numbers that are written on the page. There might be more than one. View the previous image on the website or the microfilm roll as well, even if the page you need has page numbers. View the one before that if necessary. How many different page numbers are written on the census page/image? An 1810 census entry from Bourbon County, Kentucky contained three sets of page numbers. One was stamped, one was written in ink (apparently), and another looked like it was written in pencil. And sometimes the page numbers are one every other "page." Be certain to identify the page number by describing its location (stamped upper left, handwritten lower right, etc.).

*Family of Samuel and Annie (Murphy) Neill,*

*near Stillwell, Hancock County, Illinois, early 1890s*

# Chapter 9: Portable Ancestors, First Purchases, and Cousin Ken

## Jumping the Pond too Fast

*24 September 2009*

Are you trying to cross the pond too fast? Sometimes frustration with an "I don't know where to research my German/English/Irish, etc." ancestor is because the homework has not been completely done in the area where settlement took pace. Have you looked at *everything* in the area where your immigrant ancestor settled? Everything means everything, even things you think might not help and things you need assistance accessing or understanding how to use. You never know what a document will say until you look at it. Clues can be in the most unexpected of sources. You should also research the children completely as they might have left clues as to their parents' origins. Homework, homework, homework.

## Is that Middle Name a Last Name?

*28 September 2009*

Is your ancestor's "middle" name one that could be construed as a "last" name? If so, have you searched for him (or her) in all records where he is "missing" with that middle name entered as his last name? It just might be the trick to finding him. There's also no guarantee that a middle name that's a commonly used surname is the mother's maiden name. It is a potential clue, but sometimes people are named for neighbors or famous people instead of their grandparents.

# Is Your First Guess Wrong?

*29 September 2009*

The subject line to the mailing list was "old Danish." I was slightly hungry and pastry was the first thing that entered my mind when the message crossed my path. What the writer meant was the older style of the Danish language and handwriting. In this case, the first guess just might have been because I have an odd sense of humor. Are you still operating under the assumption that your first guess about something was correct?

# Agreement Doesn't Mean They are Right

*30 September 2009*

Just because two (or even more) records agree on a fact or a date, does not mean they are correct. It just means they contain the same information. It could still be incorrect, especially if many years intervened between the date of the event and the date of the record. A death certificate, a tombstone, and an obituary may all provide the same date of birth. The most likely reason for the agreement is that they really have the same informant providing the information on all three records.

# How Portable was Your Ancestor?

*30 September 2009*

Think about your ancestor's career or occupation. How portable was it? A landowning ancestor who farmed might have moved, but it likely wasn't every two years as moving took a little bit of time and planning if your ancestor actually was a property owner. Your ancestor who was a tenant farmer may have moved if he lost his lease to the property or had difficulty paying the rent. If your ancestor had a small business, he might not have moved around too much, especially after he got himself established. However, if you ancestor had a skilled trade, he might have been able to move more quickly, assuming he could find work. And your day laborer ancestor (like a few of mine) might have moved all the time. Think about your ancestor's job, career, or employment, and how easily it might have been for him to be portable.

## The Importance of Citing as You Go

*02 October 2009*

The best time to create a citation to a record is the moment you have it. It is right there in your face, hopefully you know what it is and where you got it if you are looking right at it. And if you don't know what it is or where you got it, shouldn't you figure that out anyway?

## How Secondary is it?

*03 October 2009*

This post includes thoughts and not necessarily answers. If my daughter tells someone her date of birth, she is providing secondary information of that date. She has no firsthand knowledge of her date of birth. If I tell someone that today is my daughter's 21st birthday, is that primary or secondary information? I was present at the birth, but if I say it or write it down twenty-one years later, is that statement primary or secondary? If I write it down within a month of her birth, that probably would be considered primary information. But if I don't refer to any documents at all and write it down twenty-one years later is that still primary information? And how reliable is it? Some would say that my statement regarding her date of birth is primary because I was there when it happened and that classification of that information as primary or secondary is making no comment about the perceived reliability of that information. That's why it's important to include the informant of any information and when they provided it.

## Who Was the Informant?

*04 October 2009*

Think about that marriage record for your great-grandparents that gives the names of their parents. Think about that 1900 census form that provides the place of birth for the parents. Do you really know who provided that information? Did the bride give some of the groom's information? Did the groom provide some of the bride's information? Did the wife in a 1900 census enumeration simply guess at where her in-laws were born? Very possible. And since most of us were not there when our great-grandparents' wedding took place or when the 1900 census was taken, the only thing we can do is conjecture about who answered those questions. How would your analysis of a record change if you decided someone else was the likely informant?

## Could You Be Wrong?

*05 October 2009*

I realize it would never happen to any *Tip of the Day* readers, but could you possibly have made a mistake at some point in your research? Sometimes the mistake, while still a mistake, does not seriously impact your research or any conclusions, but in some cases it just might. While reviewing an illustration for an article I wrote years ago, and creating its citation, I realized that I had the date of marriage incorrect by two years. It was clearly just a typo and did not impact my conclusion, but it was still wrong and could actually impact the number of potential children for the couple. Could you have made a mistake or typed something incorrectly? Is it possible that the mistake has an impact on a conclusion? Just a thought. It could happen to anyone. After all, we are human!

## Stop Multitasking

*06 October 2009*

This is a concentration tip, not just a genealogy tip. Our laptop is on the fritz and my daughter wanted to use the desktop computer for some schoolwork, and so I was forced to actually read some copies of homestead case files without the internet and email as a constant distraction. Guess what? I noticed three things I had not realized the first time I read through the papers. The first time I read them had been while I was waiting on webpages or search results to load. Is multitasking your problem? Would you notice more details in a record or a file if it had your complete attention?

## Looking at Things You Have Not Really Looked at in Years

*09 October 2009*

I recently wrote about my former brick wall ancestor, Ira Sargent. One of the records mentioned was his 1900 census enumeration. I had originally looked at it years ago, probably when I was about fifteen years of age. I had seen it several times in the interim and really hadn't given it a lot of thought. A reader pointed out that part of Ira's census entry looked like it was in a different handwriting and perhaps had an item written in it after the census taker had made his enumeration. I'm not certain yet what was going on with the entry, but it makes a good point that perhaps something you've seen several times over several years may contain an anomaly that you may never have noticed. Is there something you first looked at years ago that perhaps warrants a second look?

## Do You Have It All?

*09 October 2009*

A cousin graciously shared with me a copy of a pension record a relative had shared with her. I was very glad to get it. The relative of the cousin received the file from the National Archives years ago. I wondered if the National Archives had sent her the entire file as it looked like the original copies were made in the days when mail-in requests were usually for "selected documents." Turns out there was at least one page the relative was not sent. In this case, the missing document was not a "huge" discovery, but sometimes it can be.

## Name and Location at Google Books

*10 October 2009*

When searching books.google.com, try a search for your ancestor and the county where he lived. A search for "John Rucker Orange Virginia" located several like references to my ancestor, including one in *The Colonial Churches of St. Thomas' Parish, Orange County, Virginia*. I might have eventually found the reference, but Google Books made it faster. Google Books (or any online site of digital book images) does not have everything and full-text searches can overlook references if the text was difficult to automatically read.

## Look When You Do Not Expect It

*11 October 2009*

Years ago (before I knew better) when working on my brick wall ancestor, I ignored probate records. I was always told he was "dirt poor" and I knew that truly poor people rarely have probate records. I eventually searched them anyway. He actually had two probate files—my "dirt poor" ancestor. How can you die twice and have two estates? Turns out for the time period in question, insanity cases were filed with the probate and estate records. It was two insanity cases I had located for him, not probate cases. If I had never looked in estate files, I never would have found out information about his insanity hearings.

## Get Obituaries of Aunts and Uncles by Marriage

*12 October 2009*

I was looking for information on a lady I thought was a sister of my ancestor. I requested her obituary, hoping it would provide information on her family and her origins. It listed the names of two children, but not where they lived or any other details. The obituary was full of nice, lovey-dovey sentiments, but nothing I could use to further my research. Her husband's obituary was a different story. It was full of information on his children (some of whom were with a different wife) and other details about him that might help me locate more information about the wife. Don't neglect those spouses of ancestral siblings. Their records may contain just the clue you need.

## Would a Chart or Table Help?

*14 October 2009*

When transcribing data, you want to remain as true to the original as possible. However, when analyzing data, some creativity may come in handy. Consider organizing census information in a chart or a table. This can be done using a spreadsheet or a table in a word processing document. Transcribing census information is easier using a table that parallels the enumeration. Create a blank one as a template.

There are other ways charts and tables can help with census work. Take the twenty names before and after your ancestor in the 1800-1830 census and put all of them in a table. How many names (besides your ancestor) do you see repeated? Are these names possible clues? If your ancestor migrated during those years, common neighbors are even more important as ancestral associates.

## Counties on BLM site

*14 October 2009*

When performing a land patent search on the BLM Site (www.glorecords.blm.gov), remember that the county names might have changed between the time of the patent and today. At the time the relative filed his homestead/preemption claim in 1887, his land was in Elbert County, Colorado. Today it is in Kit Carson County.

# Is That "P" Really a Double "S?"

*16 October 2009*

In older documents, many times a double "s" would be written in a way that looks like a "p" or perhaps an "f" to the unsuspecting modern eye. Consequently, my DeMoss ancestors occasionally appear in records as "Demop."

# Civil Versus Church Record of a Marriage

*17 October 2009*

Remember that if the civil record of a marriage indicates your ancestor was married by a minister, there may be a church record of the marriage as well. That record may provide additional information besides what is on the civil (government) record of the marriage, particularly if the denomination was one that tended to keep detailed records.

# Are You Missing the Obvious?

*18 October 2009*

Is it possible that the answer is staring you right in the face? Sometimes re-analyzing a document will bring the "obvious" out of the dark. Sometimes typing it will. Sometimes reading something out loud will. Sometimes having someone else look at it will make a difference. Sometimes we jump to the wrong conclusion and never really get that out of our heads.

# Learn About the Records

*19 October 2009*

Have you really learned about the records in that "new" location you just started researching? Don't assume that records in one location are the same as in another. When I started my late 1700 research in Virginia, it never dawned on me to ask for a marriage bond. I had never used them in the upper Midwest, so I never thought to ask for them when my ancestors had been traced to a new location. Had I read a basic Virginia genealogy guidebook or research outline I would have been aware of them. Laws can be different as well. Research methods are similar from one area to another, but available records can vary greatly. Now familiarizing myself with the basic sources in a new area is one of the first things that I do before I start actual research.

## Online Databases Should be Used as Clues
*20 October 2009*

What you find in someone's online genealogy compilation should be used as a clue. There's one tree on *Ancestry.com* (with over 20,000 names) that shows my great-grandparents with a child they never had. This supposed child didn't die at birth, but according to the tree lived a complete life with children of their own. I've gotten some clues from the online trees, but do not use what you see there as anything other than a hint of a suggestion.

## Land Patents at the Bureau of Land Management Site
*21 October 2009*

The website with land patents from the Bureau of Land Management site is wonderful, but there are a few suggestions and warnings. Patents represent federal land records only—the local courthouse has subsequent private transactions which may contain more information depending on the situation the precipitated the sale. Federal cash land sale file entries contain minimal information unless there is something unusual about the transaction, such as the claimant dying during the process, was actually filing a pre-emption claim, converting a homestead claim to a cash sale, etc. Patents are tagged geographically to the area where the patented land was located, not where the claimant was from or was living at the time. And if you don't know your township from your section, read their FAQ page at www.glorecords.blm.gov.

# Look it Up

*22 October 2009*

If there is a word in a document that you do not know the meaning of, look it up. Even if you think you know what the word means, you still might want to look it up, just in case. Misinterpretations can create brick walls where none existed.

# Does it Sound the Same?

*23 October 2009*

If the name as written on a document sounds like the name you are looking for, consider it to be the same name. Spellings do not have to be consistent and are notoriously incorrect. Your real work is to make certain you have the same person, not to proofread every record you discover.

# Spelling Names of Places Incorrectly

*27 October 2009*

I may be picky, but when reviewing compiled genealogy information I watch spellings of place names (especially names that are standardized like county names). If there are several errors, I get a little skeptical of the rest of the file. The occasional typo (although most software catches non-standard location names) can result from user unfamiliarity with software or typing issues, but if the database I find has some of these spellings:

- Hartford County, Maryland
- Amhurst County, Virginia
- Schuler County, Illinois

then I am a little worried about the rest of the data. Call me persnickety, but genealogy is about details. If place names that are established and standard (as these are) are not spelled correctly, how certain can I be that names, dates, and relationships are entered in the way they should be? I'm not talking about someone trying to read the name of a German town on a nearly illegible death certificate—that's something different altogether.

## Make a Chart

*28 October 2009*

Is there any way that information you are trying to analyze can be put into chart format? Think about how you could make headings and what items you should extract from each record or source to create a table. Sometimes just organizing things in a different way makes things stand out that you didn't notice before.

## Trace the Stepchildren

*28 October 2009*

In a family that seemed to be a problematic, one of the key methods to locating certain people was to trace the stepchildren of their father. Finding them lead me to information on the people for whom I was actually looking.

## Pre-Fill That Research Log

*31 October 2009*

Fill out as much of your research log as you can while you are preparing to research. This will help you prepare and a partially completed research log (with titles, etc. already filled in) will increase the chance you actually use your log as you research.

## All Names Spelled the Same?

*01 November 2009*

Do all the records you have on your ancestor have his name spelled in the exact same way? I have very few ancestors where their name is spelled the same way on each document or source. Chances are, if your ancestor's names are spelled the same way on everything you have, that you have not researched as many documents as you should have. Although Smith and Jones don't get spelled wrong too often.

## Change Jurisdictions

*03 November 2009*

If records at the county level have not brought about success, consider searching for records at the town/village level, the state level, and the federal level as well.

## From Whom was the First Purchase Made?

*05 November 2009*

If your ancestor was a landowning farmer and migrated from Point A to Point B, check to see from whom he purchased that first piece of property when he arrived in Point B. It might have been a relative or former associate, neighbor, etc. The owner of that property in Point B might have been looking to sell it and heard that his relative or former neighbor was thinking of moving. The deed won't say the buyer and seller had known each other for twenty years or were related to each other. That's not how it works. You will have to actually research them.

## Search on the Land Warrants Name Fields at BLM

*06 November 2009*

Search the Bureau of Land Management site glorecords.blm.gov/search/default.aspx for potential land warrants issued in your ancestor's name. These warrants may have been issued as patents for property in a state where your ancestor never lived, particularly if he assigned his warrant to someone else and did not patent any property himself. Warrants could also be issued in the name of the qualifying veteran's widow if the veteran died before the warrant application was filed. Don't search for warrants in the state where your ancestor lived or served from, as patents are linked to the actual location of the patented property.

## Analyzing Ages

*25 January 2010*

Think about all the different documents that list an age for your relative. Can you use those to reach any consensus about when the person was born? A chart with each document and the age it contains can help you in determining how many of these documents are consistent with each other, which ones are fairly close, and which ones are different from the rest.

## Did Cousin Ken Get the Whole Thing?

*08 February 2010*

Are you using Civil War pension papers that cousin Ken got fifteen or twenty years ago? Did he get the complete set or just the "genealogically relevant" ones? The complete set may contain information not shown in the "genealogically relevant" pages. That same concept applies to any record a relative sends you—whether you know their research skill level or you do not.

## Legal Definition

*09 February 2010*

When using a term in an old record, ask yourself if you are using the term and understanding the term in the legal context in which it was used and at the time in which it was used. Not everything is written from a 21<sup>st</sup> century perspective.

## Definition Mortgagee

*10 February 2010*

On a mortgage, the mortgagee is the person who is loaning the money and who holds the note. It might not always be a bank, it might be a family member, neighbor, etc. This could potentially be a clue to an associate of your ancestor.

## A Grantee

*11 February 2010*

On a land record, a grantee is the person who purchases, acquires, or is otherwise receiving title to real property. Read the entire deed to see exactly what sort of title is being transferred.

## A Grantor

*12 February 2010*

On a land record, a grantor is the person who sells the property or is assigning their title or interest in property to someone else. Read the entire document to see the specifics of exactly what is being transferred.

## A Warrantee (Land Records)

*13 February 2010*

A warrantee is someone to whom a warrant for land has been issued. A military land warrant generally did not transfer title to a specific piece of property, but rather indicated the holder had the right to acquire a specific amount of acreage in the federal domain. Military land warrants were issued based on military service. Just because someone got a warrant does not mean they actually settled on federal land. Military land warrants could be sold and assigned to someone else who finally obtained a specific piece of property. That person was the patentee.

## Flip it Over

*15 February 2010*

If you have a newspaper clipping that is undated and unsourced, flip it over. Anything on the back can be a potential clue as to the location or the date of the original newspaper, even classified ads. One obit I found in a set of clippings had a date, but not the name of the newspaper. Flipping it over, I found several classified ads. The street names told me it was from a nearby town of 40,000 and not one of the small towns near where the relative actually died.

*Trientje (Janssen) Ufkes [1895-1986]*

*is the woman on far right.*

*others are unidentified.*

*probably Basco, Hancock County, Illinois*

# 10 Signs You Have a Genealogy Obsession

1) You check FamilySearch four times a day every day for updated releases or databases.

2) You've grabbed a green leaf on a real tree thinking it was on your Ancestry.com page.

3) Your family takes the long way places to avoid cemeteries when you are in the car.

4) You have seriously thought about hiding in a library to get locked in after it closes.

5) You spent more searching for your ancestors 1810 tax records than you did preparing your own 2010 taxes.

6) You know more about your spouse's ancestors than you know about your spouse.

7) You would easily spend your entire vacation in a library.

8) You have already scheduled a vacation day from work for when the 1950 census is released.

9) The majority of pictures in your Facebook photo section are of people who are dead.

10) You've recognized yourself in at least half of these signs.

# Chapter 10: Dead Reasons, Getting and Giving, Just Me, and Death Names

## Are There Gaps?

*16 February 2010*

*Genealogy Tip of the* Day readers know that sometimes we miss a day with a tip and that there's a resulting gap. Those gaps make an excellent point. When viewing records that are filed chronologically, pay attention to filing dates, dates of record, page numbers, etc. Are there gaps? If so, it could indicate missing or misfiled records or pages.  Don't just look for the name of your person in the record. Look for clues that may suggest records are missing. Browsing is the best way to do that.

## Check That Date!

*17 February 2010*

For some reason, I thought today was my great-grandmother Ufkes' birthday. I am not certain where I got it in my head that her birthday was 17 February, but I did. Unless you are certain--*check*! I was partially correct--Trientje Maria Janssen was born on the 17th, but it was 17 April, not February. Memories can fail.

## Did the Reason Die with Them?

*18 February 2010*

Some events leave behind absolutely no record and those aware of it never share the story with anyone--ever. It is possible that some secrets or stories will never be uncovered. However, that does not mean we stop trying to find the answers and that we don't analyze records as completely as possible. We do. Just know that there are limitations to every search and that some people will never be found. Don't stop looking, keep learning about new sources, and keep improving your research and analytical skills.

## A Source for Every Statement of Fact

*19 February 2010*

Sometimes it is easy to criticize those who insist on a "source for every fact." However, having started to do this on a few of my lines that I have not looked at in years, I have learned one thing. It has forced me to correct many things I have either transcribed or remembered incorrectly. It may be heresy to say this, but the world won't end if your citations are not perfect. However, they should lead you or someone else back to the original. Going back and getting the actual information right may even cause you to break down those brick walls that were accidentally created by the researcher themselves. Of course, this never happens to me---just other people!

## Take a Free Trial--Some Advice

*20 February 2010*

Many genealogy pay-for sites offer free trials. Here are a few pieces of advice: Get the free trial when you will actually have time to use it. Keep track of the credit card used to "hold" or access the free trial. They will bill you if you do not contact them and have them cancel. Mark your calendar for two days before it expires. That is the day you decide. If the expire date falls on a Sunday or Saturday, always plan to call on at least the Friday before that date, preferably on Thursday. Of course, if you aren't going to cancel, then it is not a problem.

## The Getting and the Giving

*22 February 2010*

Remember that for every ancestor who owned a piece of property, there should be a deed or title transfer when the property was obtained or came into his possession. There should also be a transfer when the property left his possession. Make certain you have each one and that the total incoming acreage equals the outgoing acreage. The "leaving possession" deed might not have your property-owning ancestor's name on it: it could have been sold for back taxes, foreclosed on if a mortgage was not paid, or sold by his heirs after his death. Don't assume your city dwelling ancestors never owned any property. Even records on a small plot may be helpful.

## Get A Second Opinion

*23 February 2010*

Interpreting documents is never easy. If you have a complicated document or record, consider having more than one person interpret it. Different people can easily interpret the same thing in slightly different ways. Make certain you know something of the background of who gives you advice. Not everyone's skill levels are the same and a response from an anonymous poster on an email list or a message board may not be all that reliable and may lead you further astray.

## Underlined on a Deed?

*24 February 2010*

Is a word underlined on that deed you copied at the courthouse? Underlining was often the clerk's way of indicating that the underlined item looked odd and incorrect on the original, but that's what the document actually said. Some clerks would use similar notations such as straight lines above the word, wiggles above the word, etc. The clerk's job was to transcribe verbatim, not to fix. Fixing the document requires a lawyer and perhaps legal action.

## Write it Down Now!

*25 February 2010*

"Great-grandma Neill wouldn't let Nellie date the Humke boy because they were related." I know someone told me that. I am not dreaming it. I had already known the "Humke boy was related," but the dating (or potential dating) was news to me. I remembered the tidbit while doing something completely unrelated. The problem is that I cannot for the life of me remember who said this to me. I will write it down now and have to use myself as the source, even though I have no first hand knowledge of it myself. It is even more frustrating because I was told this little nugget years after I had started genealogy and knew the importance of writing things down as soon as possible.

## Check Around Before Buying a Copy of Any Record
*26 February 2010*

It always pays to check around before buying a copy of any record. There are times when multiple avenues to obtaining a genealogical record are available. Generally speaking, try sources in the following order:

- Family History Library
- State or Regional Archives
- Local, County, or State Record Office

Contact individuals who may have some local knowledge as well by communicating with local libraries, county historical or genealogical societies, etc. Never pay for immediate, overnight, or any speedy service to get a copy of any record. Genealogists do not need documents overnight. Considering hiring a local professional if you need a large number of records and can't get them via mail. This is meant to be general guidance only, but avoid paying exorbitant fees for "extra" services if at all possible.

## Reminder about Pronunciations

*27 February 2010*

A student asked me if I knew where "Mr. Lowrey" was. At least it sounded it like he was asking for Mr. Lowrey. It turns out his instructor's first name was Larry. And the last name was not Lowrey. Could your ancestor inadvertently have confused the census taker about what name came first and what name came last?

## Every Name on the Document

*28 February 2010*

Look at every name on every record for your ancestor. Why are those other names on the document? Names of officials and the like might not be huge clues, but they could be, and the other names might be worth investigating. Witnesses can be associates. Notaries usually have a certain area where they operate.

## A Minor Naturalization

*01 March 2010*

A minor naturalization is a naturalization in which the person who naturalized immigrated while they were a minor. It does not mean they were a minor when they naturalized. Individuals whose naturalization was a "minor naturalization" followed a different set of procedures than individuals whose naturalization was not. The reason for the difference is that when the individual arrived as a minor they were too young to swear out a declaration of intention to become a citizen upon their arrival and could perform no legal action on their own until they were of the age of majority. A minor whose father naturalized in the 19th and early 20th century usually became a citizen. All of this depended on contemporary law and practice *at the time of the naturalization*—not today.

## Every Record was Created by Humans

*02 March 2010*

Remember that every record was created by a human. Consequently, any one piece of information could be incorrect. Could that be what's causing your brick wall?

## 1855 Bounty Land Application Instructions

*03 March 2010*

We don't normally point to webpages here on *Genealogy Tip of the Day*, but among the thousands of neat things on www. archive.org is the following: *Instructions and forms to be observed by persons applying to the Pension Office for bounty land under the act of March 3, 1855 : entitled "an act in addition to certain acts granting bounty land to certain officers and soldiers who have been engaged in the military service of the United States."* The easiest way to find the item is to search for "instructions pension office 1855" on www.archive.org. This might explain some things about your ancestor's bounty land application.

## County Recorder's Miscellaneous Record Books

*05 March 2010*

County Recorder's offices typically have a series of what are called miscellaneous record books where they will record copies of things that do not fall into the typical record categories. I have seen copies in these books of:

- out-of-county divorce decrees
- out-of-county death certificates
- medical licenses
- legal agreements not related to property or real estate

One never knows what one will encounter in these records. Give them a try!

## Never Stop Learning

*06 March 2010*

The day you decide your genealogical skills do not need tweaking is the day you probably should take up a new hobby. All of us involved in genealogy should be learning something every day. Becoming a better genealogist is a daily process of growth.

## Are Employment Records the Answer?

*07 March 2010*

Do you have ancestors for whom employment records might answer some questions, or at least provide you with some information of which you were not already aware? Rural ancestors rarely have these records, but those with urban ancestors might want to see if records of their ancestor's former employers have been archived or stored somewhere. Local libraries and county historical/genealogical societies are a good place to start asking.

## Evoking Memories Through Music

*08 March 2010*

If great-aunt Myrtle is having difficulty remembering things from her past, consider downloading or getting copies of music that was popular during the time period you are trying to get her to remember. Music may be the impetus to get her memories flowing.

## It Is Not Just Me

*09 March 2010*

Years ago, I had several people in a beginning genealogy class tell me that my ancestors were unique—not everyone had ancestors who left the kinds of records mine did, and that my ancestors must have been different. I don't think so. Part of it is just how hard you look. None of my ancestors were particularly wealthy. A few lived hand-to-mouth and several barely hung on during the Depression. Yes, most were farmers, but not all were landowners, and those who were owned farms of a typical size for their era (agricultural census records are a great way to make these comparisons). My in-laws left records, too, and they were not all farmers. Even the city dwellers who didn't own their homes left records. The key is learning about all the records that might be available and being diligent. Leave no stone unturned—you might be surprised at what is out there. Most importantly, ask for help or suggestions.

## Et Al. Deeds

*10 March 2010*

Finding too many deeds for too little time when researching your ancestor at the county courthouse? When time is limited, the "Et al." deeds should be high on your priority list. "Et al" means "and others," meaning that at least one person besides your ancestor is listed on the deed. If my research time in a facility is quickly coming to an end, these are the documents I look at first. Every document that mentions your ancestor has the potential to be genealogically relevant, but when it is 3:30 pm. on a Friday afternoon and the courthouse closes at 4:00 sometimes decisions have to be made.

## No Probate Doesn't Mean No Records

*11 March 2010*

Remember that if your ancestor died and left no probate, it does not mean that there are no records settling his affairs. There may be deed or non-probate court records that effectively settled the ancestor's estate without a "probate" settlement. It pays to look.

## Boundary Changes

*14 March 2010*

Have you considered whether changes in county, township, or other boundaries are creating research headaches?

## You Never Know Until You Ask

*17 March 2010*

A Google search turned up online scans of old land patents. I clicked on the link and I was told that I needed a username and password. My budget for memberships was exhausted and I got distracted and forgot about it. A few days later I came upon the page again and decided to ask if there was any way to get temporary or "pay-perview" access for the few documents I wanted immediately. Turns out there was no fee and I was given the generic access codes. You never know until you ask.

## Sometimes There is No Answer

*19 March 2010*

Once in a while, genealogists need to remind themselves that there might not be an answer to a question. This does not mean that one does not keep looking, but that sometimes there just are not the records available to answer the question, determine the parentage, connection, etc. Sometimes realizing when you have exhausted all avenues is a good thing to know. Of course, it also might be advised to ask an expert if you really are at the end of your genealogy rope.

## Remember the Original Purpose

*19 March 2010*

It is easy for some genealogists to get lost in the research and forget the original purpose of the records we use. Deeds were to transfer real property, probates were to settle estates, courts were to settle disputes, etc. The records we use were created for a specific purpose. Remember that. It may influence how you interpret things.

## Experts Don't Always Know Everything

*20 March 2010*

No expert is perfect. No one knows everything. A well-known lecturer indicated in a handout that all land records contain a metes and bounds description that mentions lines and many times mentions neighbors. No, they do not. Legal descriptions of property in federal land states do not often mention metes and bounds unless the property lines are really convoluted, and when they do, names of neighbors aren't always mentioned. Metes and bounds are used in state land states. Turns out the "expert" had only done

East Coast research and assumed all land records were the same. There's a lesson about assumptions as well.

## Get Specific About the Occupation

*22 March 2010*

If your ancestor was a farmer, was he a farm owner, a tenant farmer, or a farm laborer? If he was a farm laborer, did he have one family for whom he worked for decades or did he work where he could as a day laborer? The differences are significant, and knowing which type of farmer he was helps indicate how mobile your ancestor likely was, what types of records he left behind, etc. Farming isn't the only occupation where these distinctions are important. Did your ancestor work in a blacksmith shop, or own his own shop? Again, the difference is important. Sometimes all we have are vague ideas of what our ancestor did—but sometimes we do have more.

## Why Did Your Ancestor "Break" the Rules?

*24 March 2010*

If possible, learn why your ancestor "broke the rules" or went against tradition. I'm not certain why my wife's Roman Catholic great-grandmother didn't have her last two children christened as infants. They went to Catholic school and someone mentioned to a nun that that weren't baptized. They were nearly seven and eight years old when they were baptized. She could easily have had them christened at birth. They were born in Chicago in the 1910s—there were plenty of Catholic churches in the area. There's a reason she didn't do it, I'm just not certain what it is.

## Have it Re-Researched?

*25 March 2010*

Is it possible that the person who said they would do a quick "lookup" for you in a certain record didn't really know what they were doing? Did they overlook it? Did they not consider all the spellings? Anyone can make a mistake. Might it be worth a second try? Please don't get me wrong, those who volunteer to do lookups do us a great service, but since they are human, every once in a while they can overlook something.

## Are You Paying Attention to the Dates on Those Records?

*25 March 2010*

Have you looked at the date the document was drawn up and the date it was recorded in the local records office? Was there a delay? Is there any significance to the date a document was executed? Fit the record into the context of the family. Had a child just reached the age of majority? Had someone recently died? There might be a reason even if it is not clearly stated.

## Make a List

*26 March 2010*

Before you start doing wildcard and other searches at an online database, make a complete list of all spelling variants of the name for which you are searching. Use this list to decide what wildcard searches need to be conducted in order to not overlook any variants. Keep a written list of search options so that searches are not missed and so you don't have to create the list again.

## Analyze Before you Search

*27 March 2010*

Are you analyzing that information you just located before you start performing searches of online databases? If you have found a census enumeration for a family, have you estimated the year of birth for everyone in the household? If you relied on an online transcription, have you determined if it was correct? Have you estimated the date of marriage for the suspected parents? These are good things to do before you start searching other records, as it allows you to compare information and reduces the chance you grab onto the wrong person as being a match.

## Are You in Isolation?

*28 March 2010*

Are you researching in complete isolation? Even if you cannot find relatives to bounce ideas off, there are genealogy societies, mailing lists, message boards, online groups, and a variety of other ways you can interact with other genealogists. Don't research in complete isolation. Discussing problems with others and sharing concerns is a great way to learn and expand your research.

## Get Past Different Spellings

*29 March 2010*

For those new to research, it is imperative to remember that last names are rarely spelled the same from someone's birth until their death. Sometimes the variants are obvious and sometimes they are not, but I'd never find the Demar family if I didn't look under Demarrah and Desmarais.

## Getting Past 1850

*30 March 2010*

One of the biggest hang-ups for new genealogists is working before the 1850 census. Try taking those pre-1850 enumerations that only list people by age category and "practicing" on a family where you have already discovered the children's names and ages with other records. See if the enumerations "fit," then expand your work to individuals where you don't have as much information on the children. It helps to practice first.

## Head of Household Might not be Oldest pre-1850

*31 March 2010*

Just remember that in pre-1850 United States census records, the oldest person might not necessarily be the head of the household who is named. If a grandparent or parent is living with the family, they might be the oldest person enumerated while the person named as the head of the household is actually someone younger.

## Dates of Execution versus Date of Recording

*02 April 2010*

Remember that the date a document is signed is the date of execution. The date a document is recorded at the appropriate office is the date of recording. There is a difference. Not every document was recorded promptly. Wills are usually recorded after someone's death. Deeds may not be recorded for years, but most are. Sometimes deeds will finally be recorded when the purchaser wants to sell the property and realizes the deed of purchase was never recorded.

## Is the Answer in a Whole Different Record?

*03 April 2010*

If you can't find an ancestor in a specific record and you think she should be there, go back and review the entries in other records or consider searching in different materials altogether. It may be that in working in those other materials that you find the clue that explains why the ancestor is missing in the record that had you stymied.

## Go to a Seminar

*05 April 2010*

Is there a one-day genealogy seminar or workshop near you? Consider going. Even if the topics do not necessarily seem like they will interest you, you might learn something. Workshops are often a good way to network with others before the lectures, during lunch, or other times. You can also volunteer to help with future workshops and maybe help choose the speaker, topics, etc. Sometimes listening to presentations outside your research experience gives you insight into your own problems.

## Ask for Help

*05 April 2010*

Whether or not there are "stupid questions" is debatable. However, if there is something about a record, a resource, or an ancestor you do not understand, consider asking someone. They may be able to point out some nuance that you overlooked that even seasoned researchers don't always see. And if it turns out you are missing something obvious, you probably won't die of embarrassment. And if you do, well, then you can ask your ancestors those questions personally.

## Make it Clear, Never Assume

*06 April 2010*

I was helping a high school classmate with her son's five-generation genealogy project. In one communication with her, I asked her if her Dad's family lived in or near Tennessee. After I hit send, I realized I should have clarified which Tennessee I was talking about. There is Tennessee the state and Tennessee the little town in the adjacent county to where we grew up. Are you being precise in your use of locations?

## How Off Are All the Ages?

*08 April 2010*

Look at every age of your ancestor in every available record? How consistent are they? Compare each and every one of them, creating a range of years in which your ancestor could have been born. Don't expect your ancestor to give ages that are precisely consistent. It won't happen.

## Do You Have the Name at Death?

*09 April 2010*

If you are looking for that female relative in a death record, Social Security Death Index, probate record, etc. remember that you need to have her last name on the day she died. If she married shortly before her death, that might be a problem. Make certain you really know the name under which she might be listed in those records created after her death.

## Newspaper Writeups

*10 April 2010*

Don't look for just births, marriages, and deaths in newspapers. There are other events in your relative's life that could result in them being mentioned in the newspaper. Were your ancestors married fifty years or more? Did one live to be a hundred? Were there other events that might have warranted mention in the newspaper (illegal activities come to mind)? Search for these events as well. One day those newspapers may be digitally scanned and full text searchable, but until then this approach might work.

## Act Professional

*12 April 2010*

Going to that local courthouse to do some family history research? Know what you are looking for and look presentable. Staff will take you more seriously if you act like you know what you are doing and are dressed reasonably well. Impressions matter. Save the workout clothes and pajamas for researching online at 3 a.m.

## Are You Proving Every Relationship as Best You Can?

*12 April 2010*

You should have some documentation, or at least a verifiable reason for every relationship between two individuals in your database. "Thinking two people are related" is not a reason.

## Proof Yourself

*13 April 2010*

Are you doublechecking information as you enter it into your genealogical database? Are you making certain those transcriptions are done correctly, word for word?

## What Is the Front and What Is the Back?

*15 April 2010*

If you are using any reproductions of original documents, be it microfilm, digital images, or photocopies, do you know what images came from the same piece of paper? It is not always clear what "front" should be paired with what "back." Sometimes it makes a huge difference in how you analyze documents, because the "back side" may indicate the legal purpose of the document, when it was filed and recorded, etc.

## Do You Know Your Geography?

*15 April 2010*

Do you really know the geography of the area in which you are working, or are you "working" from assumptions? Best to get maps, modern and contemporary, just to be certain.

## Don't Forget the State Archives

*16 April 2010*

You ancestor could easily appear in records in the state archives for the state where he or she lived. Sometimes we forget that states also kept records. In some cases, the State Archives (or whatever the state agency that archives state records is called) may have copies of county records as well and may have statewide indexes to certain vital records. Make certain you have included the State Archives in your searching.

## It Is Not All Digital

*17 April 2010*

Just remember that not every source genealogists use is online. Many books and materials have been digitized, but many have not. Make certain your search also includes materials that are only available in their original format.

## Geography is Three-Dimensional

*19 April 2010*

"Low is south and high is north." It was the essence of a misunderstanding another genealogist and I had. I referred to my "low-German" ancestors and she thought they lived in the southern part of Germany, perhaps because that was "lower" on the map. In this case, the "lower" part of Germany is near the sea. Are you interpreting things correctly? And remember, geography is three dimensional.

## When Was the Last Time You Looked?

*20 April 2010*

More and more unindexed records are going online every day. When was the last time you looked to see what was "new?" My most significant breakthrough came when I searched a previously unindexed state census that had just been released on *Ancestry.com*. Boom! There was a likely match on a person I was struggling with. I had not used the records before as I could not search the entire unindexed state. When was the last time you looked to see what was "new? "

## Would One Missed Word Make a Difference?

*21 April 2010*

Take care in transcribing documents and in using transcriptions. One missed word can make all the difference. While it is not a genealogy example, the following makes the point. "I put money in the envelope" means something different from "put money in the envelope." Think about those transcriptions you are creating and using. If someone missed a word, it could make all the difference.

## Google that Occupation

*22 April 2010*

Is there a census occupation you can't quite read or can read, but think someone dreamed it up? Google the word. You may find your answer.

## That Newspaper is Secondary

*23 April 2010*

Remember that newspaper accounts of events can easily be incorrect and that every detail should be verified with other records if possible. I've seen obituaries of the same person in different papers conflict with each other over contemporary events. The chance for error is even greater when dealing with details that took place decades before the obituary was published.

Technically it is the information in a newspaper that can be secondary. The actual newspaper itself is an original record. Microfilm or digital copies are usually exact duplicates of the original. Published newspaper extracts or transcriptions would be derivative sources.

## Look at the Search Boxes Carefully

*24 April 2010*

When using an online search interface, make certain you are interpreting all the search boxes correctly. It is very easy to get "ahead of the game" and waste time because you are not putting the correct things in the correct boxes. If you first do not find what you think you should, look at each search box and make certain you have (if appropriate) put in the correct item.

# Chapter 11: 100%, Errors, Rushing Structure, and Homemade Abbreviations

## Take a List

*25 April 2010*

If you are going to do any research in records where the use of terms is particularly important (*eg.* land records, court records, foreign language church records) take a "cheat sheet" of key terms or words and what they usually mean. It will help. For example, a sheet for land records should include grantor, grantee, quit claim, mortgagor, mortgagee, etc. A sheet for foreign language work should contain the main genealogy words in that language.

## Get a Perpetual Calendar

*27 April 2010*

They are all over the internet. When using any document or record that refers to dates, particularly one that says last Thursday, two weeks ago, etc., use a perpetual calendar to determine the actual date. A simple Google search will locate numerous online references to perpetual calendars.

## Using Maps with the Census?

*28 April 2010*

Are you using a map when you search the census for your ancestor? If you don't have appropriate, contemporary to your problem census year maps, you could easily be making mistakes or looking in places that are not quite right. With indexes, manual searches of the census are not always necessary, though sometimes they are. Maps, however, are not optional. You need to know where locations are and how they fit together.

## An Error May be an Error

*30 April 2010*

Before you analyze that incorrect marital status in a census, before you get all "fussed up" over an incorrect place of birth, consider the possibility that what is wrong is simply an error. Sometimes our ancestors do lie, but sometimes people just make mistakes. Sometimes a mistake is just a mistake. Something to think about before we go making up some grand reason behind the discrepancy.

## Could a National Event Explain Your Problem?

*01 May 2010*

My wife has an ancestor who "disappeared" ca. 1918 shortly after he and his wife had marital problems. It is possible he changed his name in order to start his life anew. It is also possible he enlisted in the service during World War I and never returned to the area where he was from (either because he died or he simply chose to live somewhere else). Another relative died in his early 30s in the 1860s. It is too early for a death certificate in that location, but I do have his estate records. Did he die in the Civil War? Keep in mind the time frame of the event. Was there some national event that could explain your ancestor's absence or demise?

## Early Years of a County

*03 May 2010*

Did your ancestor live in a county in the first years after it was formed? Is it possible the boundaries were somewhat in flux in those early years? You still might want to check the records of the "old county" for a few years after the new one was formed, just in case.

# Anglicization

*04 May 2010*

Anglicization is the process of translating a name into English. Many immigrants anglicized their names after arrival—but rarely at Ellis Island. Some non-English names could be translated. The Swedish *Anders* became *Andrew*, as did the Latin *Andreas*. For non-standard names or those that had no real translation, the ancestor might never have Anglicized or might have simply taken an English name that was "close" or began with the same initial sound or letter. Focke may have become Frank, Trientje might have become Tena, or Noentje may have become Nancy. Trientje actually has a root similar to the English-language Katherine, but most of my Trientjes who Anglicized their name opted for Tena instead. Remember that your ancestor was not a linguist, so don't over analyze that translation of his name. Sometimes their new name has little bearing to the old one—that's how Gesche became Mary.

# Never One Hundred Percent

*05 May 2010*

Keep in mind that you can never be one hundred percent certain that any one record is one hundred percent correct. There is always the chance of an error. Never "fix" what appears to be an obvious error, either. Transcribe exactly as written and put your commentary elsewhere. Your fix may not be correct.

# Take a Break

*09 May 2010*

Have you been working for too long on one family or one problem? Let it sit for a while, perhaps a week or two, and work on something else. A month away may allow you to come back with a different perspective and notice something you did not notice before.

## Never Correct an Original

*10 May 2010*

Don't correct an original when making a transcription. Copy it as it is written. If you know spellings, etc. are wrong, comment on them separately and clearly indicate that the comments are yours. Putting comments in brackets [] is an excellent idea.

## Look with the Kids

*11 May 2010*

If you cannot find an older relative in a census, make certain you have looked for all their children. They may be hiding there, perhaps with an incorrectly spelled last name that you have not thought to search for before.

## Don't Rush to Enter Family Structure

*12 May 2010*

Filing quickly is good—things get misplaced if you don't. Rushing to do your data entry (other than the basic elements of what was in the record) based upon that find may not be a good idea. Some records do not clearly indicate precise relationships. Most genealogical database programs require a specific type of relationship—you can't just say "related." Analyze what you find. Draw conclusions and determine the family structure, and then put the relationships in your database. You can enter individuals in a database program without indicating the relationship. Also make certain you have the same person before you tie that record to someone already in your database.

## Pensions of Siblings?

*14 May 2010*

Did any of your ancestor's siblings receive or apply for a military pension? If so, there's a chance your ancestor provided testimony as to service, marriage, or other information.

## How is it Similar—How is it Different?

*14 May 2010*

When a record is located, try to compare it to other records of the same type or in the same series. Don't just look at the record you found in isolation from others in the same set. How is the record for your relative different from other records? How is it similar? Some differences, such as name, date, etc. identify the record as being for your ancestor as opposed to someone else, but make certain the "boilerplate" of the document is the same as others in the series. Differences, such as a phrase or word that does not appear in other documents, may indicate a clue. There's a reason for the difference. Analyzing a record in comparison to others is especially helpful when looking at church records, which often are kept in loose paragraph format before standard forms were used.

## Have You Considered More than One Relationship?

*16 May 2010*

Is it possible that two individuals who were first cousins were actually cousins on another side of the family as well and were related in multiple ways? It happens. Many of my maternal relatives are related to me in more than one way. It is not unusual for someone to be my second cousin, my third cousin, and my fourth cousin. Individuals who are related by blood may have additional non-biological relationships as well, either by marriage, employment, etc. Sometimes the connections are not entirely crystal clear and may be multi-layered.

## Going to the Remote Courthouse

*17 May 2010*

When visiting that distant courthouse, remember that the purpose of the office is to do regular daily business, which often is not to assist you with your genealogical research. Be polite, be patient, know what you are looking for, and don't come across as the "tourist genealogist" who thinks they "know everything." Your goal is to get records—remember, you most likely don't know anyone there, aren't a local taxpayer, aren't a local voter, etc. You'll have more luck with a soft-shoe approach than a brash one.

## Feme Covert

*18 May 2010*

A *feme covert* is a married woman whose rights are incorporated into those of her husband. She doesn't have legal rights of her own.

## Feme Sole

*19 May 2010*

Historically, a *feme sole* was a woman who was authorized by law to manage her own affairs. She might have been single, a widow, an abandoned wife, or in very unusual circumstances, a married woman.

## Dower

*20 May 2010*

A wife's dower is that portion of a man's estate or possessions that the law assigns to his wife, typically a third. This was determined by state statute. Dower has been abolished in the United States.

## Alternate Surnames

*21 May 2010*

If the last name is MacDonald, look for Donald. If the last name is DeMoss, look for Moss. If the last name starts with an "O," drop it.

Try looking for Wall instead of Van de Wall. On the reverse side, if the last name is Neill, you might want to try O'Neill or McNeill. After all, every Neill is an Irishman and needs to have an "O" in front of his name.

## Same Old Sources?

*22 May 2010*

If you are stuck on an ancestor, are you using the "same old sources" you always use? Are there records you avoid because you don't understand, they are "difficult" to access, etc.? Some individuals avoid land records, court records, and other records for these reasons. Are there un-utilized sources that might have the answer to your problem?

## Are You Using Only Records That Have Every Name Indexes?

*24 May 2010*

Keep in mind that there are a variety of records that might mention your ancestor and that are not every name indexed. Court records, estate records, and other records usually are not full name indexed, unless they have been abstracted and published. It may be necessary to get away from indexed records in order to solve your problem. When using any index, determine what names from the records were included in that index.

## Who Paid the Taxes?

*25 May 2010*

If you are trying to determine when an ancestor died in an era before good death records, consider looking at real property tax records if the ancestor owned real property. If the ancestor suddenly is listed as "deceased" or "the estate of," that could be a big clue as to when he died. The estate may be paying taxes for several years before the property actually changes hands, and there may be a notation as to the exact person who paid those taxes. Chances are it is a relative or someone with an interest in the estate.

## Was That Their Real Last Name?

Is the last name you think is your ancestor's last name the last name of her father or actually that of her stepfather? Perhaps the mother's remarriage is creating a roadblock for you. Was your ancestor adopted (officially or unofficially) and had varying last names in different records for that reason?

## Not Always Obvious

*27 May 2010*

Just remember what is obvious to you might not be obvious to everyone else. And that what is "obvious" to you might not even be true!

## No Homemade Abbreviations

*28 May 2010*

Use abbreviations in your records rarely. They should not be used in your transcription of a document unless they are used in the original document itself. Will anyone else know what your home-grown abbreviations mean? Will you remember them in five or ten years?

## Temporary Landing Spot

*29 May 2010*

Did your immigrant family have a temporary landing spot when they immigrated? Even if they lived in one state for thirty or forty years after their immigration doesn't mean that was where they originally settled. I had one family where many extended family members immigrated over a fifteen-year period. Almost all of them spent a few years in Kentucky before settling permanently in

Illinois. I had assumed all their records were in Illinois, but they left a significant number of courthouse documents in Kentucky—their initial landing spot.

## We Don't Have Any Relatives

*30 May 2010*

Don't assume those stories about having "no relatives" are true. One family insisted our branch was the only one to come out west to Illinois from Ohio. Turns out there were three first cousins and two aunts and two uncles of the migrating couple who also came to Illinois from the same area. Why descendants insisted we were the "only ones" is beyond me, but they were incorrect. My family lived close enough to most of their relatives from "back home" to be aware of their existence and actually bought their first piece of property in Illinois from a cousin.

## Before You Make Copies from that Book

*01 June 2010*

Don't just copy one page from a printed reference in which your relative's name appears. Copy sufficient preceding pages so the information is not viewed out of context. It may be helpful to copy the preface of the book as well, and always copy the title page so you know where you obtained the material. If you don't want to make paper copies, take digital images of all those pages.

## Try Again

*01 June 2010*

Even if you think you've tried a research approach and it was unsuccessful, try it again. I can't remember the number of times someone told me they had "searched for that," "tried that," etc. with no luck, and when we did it together the result was found. No guarantees, but maybe you need to try searching something again. It is always possible to overlook something the first time or not to search in the way you thought you did. Keeping a research log is helpful for this reason, but sometimes double checking is advised.

## An Undivided ¼ Interest. . .

*02 June 2010*

A participant on my Salt Lake City research trip found a deed that indicated the grantor was selling an undivided ¼ interest in a piece of property. This warranted further research in land and probate records. An undivided interest of this type frequently indicates some type of inheritance was involved. Not always, but often. The person holding the ¼ undivided interest in, say, forty acres, did not have a specific ten acres. Instead they had a ¼ share of the entire forty acre parcel.

## Is the Preface Correct?

*05 June 2010*

Genealogists with experience tell newer researchers to always read the preface of a book to determine what records were used, etc. This is an excellent idea. Remember, though, that the preface itself can contain errors. I once spent hours trying to locate the original record used to compile a print book based upon incorrect information in the preface.

## The Importance of Writing

*08 June 2010*

Writing up your genealogy research is important. It will make you look more closely at what you have, your assumptions, and your conclusions. Remember to write for someone who does not know anything about your family. You might be surprised at the things you learn or realize you don't know when you go to organizing your information and thoughts for someone else to read. Consider submitting your finished product to a local genealogical or historical society quarterly in the area where your ancestor lived. It is a great way to preserve your research. Don't forget to cite your sources.

## One Link at a Time

*08 June 2010*

Since my recent breakthrough at the Family History Library, I discovered an online posting about my newfound ancestor that lists dozens of his ancestors, including one on the *Mayflower*. It is important not to get too excited about these supposedly huge discoveries and take the time to prove every link in the chain. Online materials, especially those that are unsourced or that only have filenames like "jones.ftw" as sources, should be used as guides, not gospel.

## It Is Quit Claim, Not Quick Claim

*09 June 2010*

A quit claim deed is one where someone (the grantor) gives up whatever claim they have to a piece of property. They aren't guaranteeing they have title—they are just giving up their claim. A quit claim deed may have been drawn up quickly (and was usually cheaper to draw up than a deed where the grantor's ownership and right to transfer is guaranteed), but there's no such thing as a quick claim deed. It is just a mispronunciation of quit claim.

## Use Color

*11 June 2010*

I've been analyzing some census records for an upcoming article. I did the analysis with paper and pencil. What I needed was colored pencils. Then I could use the colors to mark each person and identify them by color. This would have helped me to keep them straight in my head. In a larger family, colors could be used to denote generations of descent from the first ancestral couple. There are a variety of ways that color could be used to mark up charts and other outlines you have made in your genealogy research.

## Read that County History

*13 June 2010*

Even if you can't read the entire thing, at least read the history of the town or township where your ancestor settled. Don't just look in the index or do a text search for the names of interest, actually read part of it. You may actually learn something that helps your research, including where initial settlers came from, what brought them to the area, reasons some left, etc.

## Practice at Home

*15 June 2010*

If you are going to use a digital camera to take pictures of tombstones, documents, etc. on a research trip, practice using the camera at home before you leave. Try different kinds of books, different lighting, different times of day, etc. and see what works for you and what doesn't. The place to learn about photographing items (particularly tombstones) is at home when you have time, not a thousand miles away from home on the last day of your research trip with your spouse in the car threatening divorce.

## Get off the Main Migration Routes

*17 June 2010*

Some of our ancestors migrated along paths that thousands of Americans took, but they all didn't settle along these national roads. They went where they knew people, or had a "connection" to a job, a farm, etc. The fact that your ancestor might have travelled part of the way on a common pathway might help solve some problems, but the larger problems will be solved by determining who else travelled with him from point A to point B.

## Double Check

*20 June 2010*

When entering dates into any database, check them twice. There is always the possibility that you copy something incorrectly and you may make an inconsistency where there really is not one.

## Write Down Your Thought Process

*21 June 2010*

Do not always assume you will remember why you reached a certain conclusion. In analyzing an 1870 census entry, I made some preliminary conclusions about the oldest female in the household. In reviewing the material later, it took me another ten minutes to "re-reach" those conclusions. It would have been easier if I had taken the time to write down my thoughts the first time in my notes on that specific person.

## One Census Can Easily Be Wrong

*22 June 2010*

It can be difficult to make headway when you only have one census enumeration to tell you anything about an ancestor. I was working on a Benjamin Butler, who was first located as living in Iowa in 1870. The problem was that his place of birth in 1870 (Canada) did not match his place of birth when he was finally located in 1880—that gave New York State as his place of birth. And his 1880 enumeration had him listed as William instead of Benjamin. Fortunately, the name of his wife and the remaining children in the household matched (the family was found by searching for the children and not Benjamin). When using just one enumeration to search for others, consider that any one piece of information you think you know could easily be incorrect. Wrong information impacts your search.

## Tax Lists Just Aren't for Real Property

*23 June 2010*

Remember that tax lists are not just for those who had real property. In some areas during some time periods, certain items of personal property were also taxed. Your non-landowner relatives might be listed. In some places, paupers were listed as well. These records may be kept in the same physical volume with the real estate taxes, the personal property taxes, and the paupers all listed separately.

## Why One Dollar?

*28 June 2010*

Why would an ancestor give a child $1 (or another token amount) in a will? Often this is to show that the child had not been left out. The child could have had a falling out with their parent and the token amount was the result of those issues. Perhaps the parent had already given them their inheritance, perhaps when they got married, started some type of business, bought their first farm ground, moved west, etc. In some cases, the parent may mention that a certain child has already received a sum of money and that's the reason for the token amount or no amount at all. The will may provide no reason for the token amount. The individual who was left out or given a token amount likely knew the probable reason even if it is not specifically stated.

## Google Them All Periodically

*29 June 2010*

It never hurts to do it every so often. I googled the name (including maiden name) of a first cousin of my great-grandfather. The first cousin had to have died at least forty years ago. However, the search turned up an obituary for a daughter who died in 2007!

# It Won't Be 100%

*30 June 2010*

Rarely are two separate documents 100% consistent regarding the same pieces of information. While it does happen, the more likely situation is that documents are fairly consistent with minor differences. It is up to the thorough researcher to determine if the inconsistencies are inconsequential and to find reasonable, plausible explanations for them. Violations of the laws of biology and physics should not be necessary to explain discrepancies. Years of birth for individuals can easily vary within a five-year time span, particularly for individuals born in the early 19th century and before.

# Remember the Lines

*03 July 2010*

Do you know where the lines are? The county line, the property line, the village line? If you aren't aware of where the various lines are located, are you certain you are looking in the right place? And remember that the lines can change, especially when a region is newly settled.

# Did History Make Your Ancestor Move?

*04 July 2010*

The American Revolution caused some residents of the United States to move to Canada. While not all of us have Loyalist ancestors, it is important to remember that historical events of all types might have caused our ancestors to move. Our ancestors didn't even have to be politically inclined for historical events to cause them to move.

# Anyone Can Have It

*05 July 2010*

Is there a family bible or other heirloom you'd like to at least see from your family's past? Keep in mind that any of your great-great-

great-grandmother's descendants could have it. Things didn't just pass to your immediate family. Get out and get looking. There may be thousands of people who could possibly have what you are looking for.

## A Grain of Salt

*06 July 2010*

Just a reminder to doublecheck any information you find on the Internet. Anyone can post anything. Same thing goes for "free" advice, articles, etc. Sometimes it may be on the mark and other times it may be woefully incorrect.

## Sometimes Different Names are Different People

*07 July 2010*

Years ago, I had a researcher search for the marriage of William Newman and Rebecca Tinsley in Rush County, Indiana. The couple married there in the 1830s. The researcher sent me the marriage record of Thomas Newman and Polly Tinsley who also married there in the 1830s, telling me that often times people used nicknames and that since the last names matched and the time period was right it was the same couple. Being young and inexperienced (I was probably fourteen at the time), I believed her. Later, I found out that Thomas and Polly were a separate couple, but the researcher was close. Thomas was William's brother and Polly was Rebecca's sister. Sometimes close is not close enough.

## Relationships

*08 July 2010*

Remember that in census records, relationships are given in relation to the head of the household—typically the husband. His children may not all be children of his current wife, and individuals listed as his children may actually be his stepchildren. There are also exceptions where the husband is not enumerated as the head of the household. Note carefully who is enumerated as the household head. Relationships to the head of household may change from one enumeration to another, especially if the household is made up of children of the husband, children of the wife, and children they had together. It is always worth remembering that the census is a snapshot of a household at one moment in time.

*Neill-Rampley Reunion,*

*West Point, Hancock County, Illinois, 1930s.*

*Don't use paper clips on pictures and*

*identify as soon as possible.*

## Chapter 12: Spousal Origins, Patronyms, and Death Causes

## Whose Version?

*11 July 2010*

Whose version of a story are you getting? Grandma most likely is telling you the version of events through her eyes. If she was personally involved in the situation or was particularly close to one family member who was, could she possibly be tweaking a few details or leaving something out? It's also worth considering whether Grandma ever knew the entire story to begin with. She may only be telling you what someone told her.

## Try a Different Site

*12 July 2010*

I've spent some time trying to find a "new" ancestor in any census before 1870. After a while of using *Ancestry.com,* I searched for him on *FamilySearch*. An 1850 census reference was located there that was not found on *Ancestry.com*. It still may not be my person, but it was a "hit" that for some reason I had not located before. Different sites have their own indexes (at least sometimes) and their interfaces and searches may work differently. If someone cannot be located in one index, determine if other indexes have been created for those records.

## Did you Proofread?

*13 July 2010*

Always double check those transcriptions you create of handwritten records. There's always the chance you could make a mistake. This tip came about after reading tips for the past two weeks—I found two typos!

## Just Initials?

*14 July 2010*

If you can't find your ancestor in the census with names, have you tried just initials? That's how some of my ancestors are listed in 1880.

## Transcription or Extract?

*16 July 2010*

Do you know the difference between a transcript and an extract? A transcript copies information or a record verbatim, while an extract takes out what the extractor sees as key points. If you are using published records, do you know if you have an extract or an abstract? It does make a difference.

## Look for the Hidden Clues

*17 July 2010*

Does a person providing testimony in a court case indicate that he has known your ancestor for fifteen years? Where was your ancestor fifteen years before the court case? Could you search for the person providing testimony in an attempt to try to find the ancestor? What was the connection between the ancestor and the person giving testimony? Always think about the implications of any statement you read. There may be more there than just what it says on the surface.

## Study the Church

*18 July 2010*

We're not trying to convert readers with this tip, but what do you know about your ancestor's religious affiliation? For some, the church was extremely important to them and influenced many decisions in their lives—who they married, where they settled, whether they disowned their children, etc. Is your ancestor migrating with members of a specific denomination? Did they cut off ties with a family member who left the church? Was there a church newspaper that might have mentioned your ancestor? Are all of your ancestor's associates members of that denomination? Did your ancestor "get religion" and distance themselves from their family, perhaps physically, emotionally, or both? There could be clues there.

## Get Multiple Versions

*19 July 2010*

Verifying family stories can often be difficult and the best advice is to record them as stories you were told, as they were told to you, and indicate who said them. Save your analysis and critique for later. Remember to get as many different perspectives and versions as you can. Even in one family, different children usually had different experiences with living family members and may remember things differently. Younger children may have met relatives that older ones did not, or it may have been the other way around, and their mother (or father) might have shared stories with one child and not with another.

## Abbreviated Names

*20 July 2010*

Don't forget when searching indexes to enter Wm. for William, Jno. for John, Th. for Thomas, etc. Also consider transcription variations on these abbreviations as well. If Wm. is misread, the transcribed name in the index may look nothing like William.

## There is No Such Thing as Completely Consistent

*21 July 2010*

Records will not be entirely 100% consistent. This is particularly true for records that provide "extremely secondary information" (e.g. places of birth for parents on their child's death certificate when the child dies at the age of 80). One must aim for relative consistency and when there are discrepancies, try to find an explanation for them. In the case of birthplaces, it often is because the family lived there for a time, the boundaries were changed, etc. It is also possible the informant was unaware of the correct location and just made it up or guessed. They may have also been emotionally distraught when filling out the death certificate.

## Have You Reviewed Your Proof?

*22 July 2010*

Is there a family or a problem you "solved" a while ago? Have you looked at your analysis since? Is it possible that you were wrong, your research was incomplete, or you were just in "la-la-land" when you reached your conclusion? Keep in mind that everyone is wrong once in a while. A distant relative made me go back and re-visit some research I did years ago, and while I'm not 100% certain what's "right" yet, there are some holes in what I did and I need to spend some more time reviewing the analysis. It doesn't hurt to occasionally go back and review what you thought was "done."

## Before Hiring A Professional

*23 July 2010*

Before hiring anyone to do any research for you, make certain you have thoroughly reviewed and organized what information you have. You may find you already have the answer or realize where you need to go without hiring someone. And if you do hire someone, they'll want your material organized anyway before they start.

## Nothing is 100% Complete

*25 July 2010*

Just remember, no series of documents is perfect. People die without death certificates, individuals are omitted from the census, records get filed incorrectly. Some records have more problems with accuracy than others. Keep this in mind when using any series of records.

## Frontier Research is Different

*25 July 2010*

Research in the early days of settlement of any area is difficult. Mainly this is because fewer records were kept, recordkeeping may have been less organized, people were more mobile, people were concerned with surviving and not leaving a record behind of their existence, etc. As a result, frontier research requires more analysis and patience than later research, and it also requires the researcher to locate just about everything they can get their hands on particularly when few records are available.

## Is State Law Playing a Role?

*26 July 2010*

Remember that state statutes dictate how inheritances work, particularly when a person dies without descendants of their own. What happened in 1920 might not be what happened in 1820, even if your family lived in the exact same location for the entire duration. Changes in intestate inheritance can easily be different as ancestral residences cross state lines. Reading up on state statute or asking someone with more experience with the records may be in order.

## Don't Correct

*27 July 2010*

Never correct a document when transcribing it. If you must, make an annotation separately, clearly indicating it is your annotation and not a part of the original. Don't add to the confusion. What you think is wrong may be right. If you have the urge to correct errors, there are better places to do it.

## Where Spouses Come From

*28 July 2010*

The majority of times (especially when transportation was limited), marriage partners came from:

- church
- neighbors
- others in same social class, same ethnic/cultural group, etc.

While there are always exceptions, the majority of times husbands and wives shared some of these characteristics. Keep this in mind when trying to locate spouses and marriage records of family members.

## Spell it Right

*29 July 2010*

Remember when entering your place names to spell the names of standard locations correctly. Names of towns or counties may change and may occasionally have an alternate spelling—strive to use the standard version. There are plenty of online atlases and maps that can help you out with this. Remember, it is:

- Culpeper, not Culpepper;
- Fauquier, not Fauquire;
- and Harford (MD), not Hartford—that's in Connecticut.

If your spellings of standard locations are incorrect, some may wonder about other details you have in your records. You may get a history lesson when learning the correct spelling.

## Widows Versus Veterans

*30 July 2010*

Widows of the War of 1812 were allowed to apply for bounty land in the 1850s, but not a pension until much later. If your veteran survived until the 1870s, he might have applied for a pension. Two bounty land acts in the 1850s gave most veterans (or their heirs) living in that time a total of 160 acres. I've been working on a bounty land application from the 1850s for a Kentucky widow. The actual property was patented in two separate parcels (one in Iowa and one in Illinois) by men who purchased the warrant from the widow after it had been issued. She had to prove her husband's service and her marriage to him to qualify for the warrant.

## Does it Apply Everywhere?

*31 July 2010*

When someone gives you advice, make certain it is applicable to where and when you are actually researching. Recently a poster to a mailing list made generalizations about a certain type of record. What he said is true about New England, but it's not true about points west of the former Northwest Territory. Consequently, if I were researching in Kansas and used his approach, I would be confused. The problem is that some people don't know their knowledge only applies in certain places or are unwilling to admit that they don't know everything. Genealogy is sort of like the human body—you don't treat a scratch on your little toe the way you would one on your eye.

## How Late Can You Go?

*01 August 2010*

If you don't know when someone died, have you gone through every document on them in order to determine the last date they were listed as being alive? It might be when they witnessed a document, appeared in a biography, wrote their will, signed a bond, appeared in a census, etc. Any one of a number of records might tell you "how late you can go?" But make certain the reference to them actually means they are deceased. A biography that appeared in a county history could have been published after they were dead even if the biography does not refer to them as deceased.

## Discuss It

*02 August 2010*

Discuss your genealogical problem with someone else with an interest in genealogy. They might have a different idea, see a hole in your research, or know of someone else who might be able to help. And sometimes just discussing something makes new ideas and errors easier to see than they were before even if the person to whom you are talking is unable to help.

## Change in Mindset

*03 August 2010*

While there are aspects of genealogical research that are the same across time periods, certain things are different. Different time periods and locations require different approaches despite what some may think. Researching a European immigrant ancestor to an urban area in the late 1800s is different from researching an immigrant to upstate New York in the early 1700s. If you are approaching both problems the same way, that might be adding to the confusion.

## Did They Even Know Their Age?

*04 August 2010*

It's possible that your ancestor did not even really know how old she was. A deposition in a Civil War pension file I recently obtained begins with the individual stating that they aren't really certain how old they are but they are probably in their early fifties. Did your ancestor know when they were born? Are you assuming that they did?

## A Patronym

*08 August 2010*

A patronym is a last name for someone derived from the first name of their father. For instance, Anders Swanson has sons with the last name of Anderson. Anderson would be a patronym. If Gerd Hinrichs' children use the last name of Gerdes, Gerdes would be a patronym. Johnson means "son of John," etc.

## Is the Time and Place Right?

*09 August 2010*

Do you have the right place for the right time in your genealogy database? An online tree for a relative indicates one of their ancestors was born in "Plymouth, Mass in 1600." Seems a little bit odd to me. Double check that your locations and dates are correct within the historical time frame.

## Look at the Dower Releases

*13 August 2010*

Does your ancestor have a series of deeds where he sells land over time? Have you looked closely at the place where the widow releases her dower? Is it the same wife every time? Might be a clue to multiple spouses.

## Cause of Death on Death Certificate

*14 August 2010*

Remember that what "killed" your ancestor might not be what actually killed him. Look for the secondary cause of death on the death certificate—that might have been the lingering illness that really was the culprit. Kidney failure might have been the result of something else. Don't ignore those other illnesses listed on the death certificate if you are looking for your family's medical history.

## 1840 Census

*15 August 2010*

Don't forget when using 1840 US census enumerations to look at both the left-hand page and the right-hand page. The left-hand page contains the name of the head of household and age categories for household members. The right-hand page contains the number of slaves, information on individuals engaged in various types of employment (categories only, no names), and names of Revolutionary War pensioners. There might be a big clue hiding on the right-hand page of that census—don't forget to look, Revolutionary War grandpa might be living with the family and listed—or Grandma if she was a pensioner.

## Index Missed It?

*16 August 2010*

Have you considered the possibility that the indexer missed something when creating the index? It might be that the only way to be certain the name is not in the record is to look page by page.

## Multiple Record Transcriptions

*17 August 2010*

There are several counties in Kentucky where different individuals have transcribed the local marriage records. Different people read things differently. I went through both sets of transcriptions. Good thing I did. The name of a husband of a relative was transcribed in two significantly different ways. One was so far off that I did not locate the reference in the transcription. Fortunately, the second reference was more accurate and helped me find more materials. If there are duplicate sets of transcriptions for a record, use both, particularly if the originals are not at your disposal.

## Looking for Ancestral Signatures?

*18 August 2010*

There are several places where you could locate signatures of your ancestor. Two good places are packets of estate papers (for receipts, the actual will, etc.) and actual pension or bounty land applications. Estate papers would be (usually) a county level record and pension/bounty land applications are typically a federal record (except for Confederate pensions given by states). Record copies of wills and deeds do not typically include actual signatures.

# Think Where?

*19 August 2010*

If you are looking for a specific piece of information, ask yourself, "where could that be written?" Don't focus initially on locating a birth record, instead think where could information about the birth be written? (This might be a birth certificate, newspaper announcement, family bible, etc.) Then try to access those sources. Not all of them will be equally reliable, but one of them may provide enough information to lead you to a more reliable source.

# Try All Newspaper Locations

*21 August 2010*

When looking for that relative's obituary, look in more than one location. Try where they were living when they died, where they were born, where they lived the bulk of their life, and where their children were living at the time of their death. You might be surprised where an obituary pops up. Of course, there may be no obituary at all. There's no law that says you have to have an obituary.

# Maybe You Have Exhausted All Sources

*22 August 2010*

Sometimes we need to admit that we've reached the end of our research on a particular person or a particular lineage. Maybe records have been destroyed or were not even created during the time period we need. Maybe your ancestor changed his name and the original version simply will never be known. There are situations where, unless new records are discovered or finding aids are created, research will reach a standstill. Most of my German relatives can be traced to the beginning of the Protestant church records and that's it. My Irish lines are stuck in the early 19th century because there are no more records. It's worth asking, looking, and getting advice, but it may not change the situation. Sometimes it's good to know when there's just no more you can do.

The problem is that sometimes we reach that conclusion before we should.

## Living Relatives?

*24 August 2010*

Are there any living relatives you haven't yet talked to with your family history questions? Remember that cousins, near and distant, may have family items or memories that you don't.

## Be Careful Inputting Relationships from Obituaries

*26 August 2010*

Be careful using relationships from obituaries as your sole source of information for your database. Modern obituaries especially may:

- **not mention** all children;
- **not distinguish** children from stepchildren;
- **not indicate** which spouse was the parent of which children.

Any of these things can confuse later genealogists if you assume an obituary was entirely correct. Best bet is to transcribe it (or scan it) and look for other materials to back it up.

## Recorded Their Discharge?

*27 August 2010*

Many soldiers recorded a copy of their discharge papers in the county in which they were living when they enlisted or where they lived right after their discharge. If you can't find military information on your ancestor, see if they recorded a copy of their discharge papers at their local county recorder's office.

## Join a Local Genealogical Society

*30 August 2010*

Interacting with other online genealogists is great, but face to face interaction can be good as well. Consider joining and becoming involved in your local genealogical society, even if you have no ancestors where you live.

## Coming of Age?

*02 September 2010*

In one family that I've worked on for some time, I realized that the stepchildren separated from the stepfather about the time some of them reached the age of majority. Separation is the right word as the stepfather and his minor children moved to Canada, while his stepchildren stayed in Iowa. Some of the stepchildren did not really know their biological father as he died when they were under the age of five. Their mother died shortly after the birth of her second child with the stepfather. I'm not certain exactly what went on, but I'm inclined to think that since some of the stepchildren were "of age" at the time the stepfather moved to Canada they all remained together in Iowa instead of moving with their stepfather.

## Moved Back?

*03 September 2010*

Did you ancestors "head west" for a better life only to "head back east" when things didn't pan out (literally in some cases)? Not everyone who went west stayed. Is it possible that during that short time you cannot find your ancestor in Ohio, it is because he was in California, Oregon, etc.? That may explain that one census where you cannot locate your relatives.

## Ethnic-Based Genealogy Mailing Lists

*04 September 2010*

If you are unfamiliar with researching members of your ancestor's ethnic group, considering joining a mailing list (or Facebook group, etc.) specifically for individuals researching people from that region. Networking with others who have ancestors from the same area can be extremely helpful even if they are not related.

## Older Immigrants

*05 September 2010*

Don't assume that your sixty-something ancestor would never have immigrated. If all their children had left the old country, it's very possible that Grandma or Grandpa (or both) got on the boat with the last child instead of being left in the homeland all by themselves.

## Go Back?

*06 September 2010*

Revisit repositories, libraries, websites, etc. that you've not visited in a while. They may have cataloged new materials, created new indexes, or acquired new materials since your last visit.

## After the Widow Died

*07 September 2010*

I'm working on a case where the husband's probate in the 1880s doesn't tell me very much. The widow survived. What I need to do is:

- Search for a probate/will for the wife.
- See if there are settlement deeds for any real estate after her death.
- Check for court action of non-probate courts in case there was an estate squabble after her death.
- See if she remarried and research the subsequent husband.

The problem may also be that there just wasn't anything left to settle after her death. Poor people don't leave many records.

## Check All Levels

*08 September 2010*

When searching for materials in the Family History Library Card Catalog, make certain you have searched for materials cataloged at all jurisdictional levels, not just the town. In some areas, this may include township, county, state, province, nation, etc. Don't just look at the town or village level records. There may be other available materials.

## How Accurate Did It Need to Be?

*10 September 2010*

Think about the record you are using and the pieces of information it contains. Are there facts that don't really need to be accurate given the purpose of the record? A recent tip mentioned that a marriage date may be included in a divorce record. In most divorce cases, is it material if the date of marriage is slightly incorrect or off by a day or two? It likely has no impact on the proceedings. Even a date that's further off likely is not a concern *for the case at hand*. The key fact is that the couple is married. That's the issue. Usually a date being slightly off is not going to impact the divorce case in any significant way. Keep the intent of the document in mind when analyzing the information is contains. It doesn't mean things have to be wrong, but there may be certain facts that don't have to be 100% precise.

## Analyze the Divorce Testimony Witnesses

*11 September 2010*

If your ancestor divorced, determine any relationships with those who provided testimony. Siblings and relatives may provide testimony in a divorce case without specifically stating their relationship.

## Never Moved but Changed Addresses?

*12 September 2010*

Is it possible that your ancestor never moved, but where he lived changed? In early days of settlement, county boundaries were sometimes in flux. And in urban areas, street names or numbers sometimes changed as occasionally did city boundaries. Was your ancestor annexed? Just something to think about.

## A Hidden Spouse?

*13 September 2010*

I'm not talking about one hiding in the basement. Does a man have both a first and a second wife named Mary? In locations where marriage records are not extant or are incomplete, determining multiple marriages for men can be a problem. Both wives usually assumed their new husband's last name at marriage, and if the first name of both wives are the same, the researcher may not notice (especially if the new Mary and the old Mary were about the same age). Make certain that as many details about the wife are as consistent as possible in all the records you have located.

## Read the Whole File

*14 September 2010*

Make certain you read the entire set of court, probate, divorce papers, etc. There may be incomplete or incorrect information in one part of the file that may be corrected or discussed in more detail in a later section. Viewing the documents in chronological order can be helpful and it may be to your advantage to read any conclusions or decisions first to get a better overview.

## Double Check

*15 September 2010*

Catalogers make mistakes when going through materials. They are human. Mistakes are easier to make when original manuscript materials are being catalogued instead of standardized records. Consequently, what appears as the description in the card catalog for an item can be incomplete or wrong. Items get missed when being microfilmed or digitized. Look at page numbers and dates of entries, could some be missing? And before one gets too judgmental about cataloging errors, keep in mind all those entries you used that were correct. We tend to remember those instances when something is wrong instead of all those other instances when it is right.

*Riley Rampley (1835-1893)*

## Chapter 13: Validation, Copyright, Life Estates

## Learn Something New Everyday

*16 September 2010*

Try a new genealogy website, read a how-to article from a journal, or work on a family you've never worked on before. Keep your genealogy mind engaged. Get off the cycle of searching for the same names in the same places in the very same ways. Getting outside your comfort zone may help you break down that brick wall.

## How Was Life Different?

*18 September 2010*

If you're stuck on an ancestor, make a list of ten ways your ancestor's life was different from yours. These ways can include lifestyle, educational level, ethnic background, native language, physical environment, what they likely ate for supper, etc. It just might get you thinking.

## How Was Life the Same?

*19 September 2010*

Yesterday's tip was "how was life different?" for your ancestor. Also think about what aspects of your ancestor's life were the same as yours. There has to be something. Think about what motivates you, what tasks you have to perform every day, every week, etc. Which ones did your ancestor have to perform as well? Any clues in those tasks? Any clues in those motivations? In some ways we aren't all that different from our ancestors.

## Do Your Interview Questions Suggest Answers?

*20 September 2010*

When asking relatives questions, try to avoid planting ideas in the mind of the person who is answering your questions. Do not lead the witness. You want the interviewee to remember as much as they can. Suggesting answers might cause them to "agree" with you when they shouldn't. Of course, ask for clarification if necessary, to make certain you interpreted them the way they intended. Asking if you heard correctly is different that suggesting an answer in the first place.

## Validate—Don't Just Copy!

*21 September 2010*

Use compilations of others as clues, not as proven facts to be copied down with nary a thought. Make certain you reduce the chance that you perpetuate the mistakes of others by trying to validate their conclusions and information.

## In Book Form?

*22 September 2010*

Don't assume no one has ever published part of your family history. A little searching located a genealogy published in 1987 on the family of my great-grandfather's sister's husband. It contained pictures and a great deal of information I did not have. Search out the in-laws.

## Read the Newspaper on that Day

*23 September 2010*

Need some perspective on your ancestor? Try reading a local and national newspaper on the day she was born, died, married, etc. While not every national or world event impacted your ancestor, reading the newspaper might bring some additional thoughts to your research. And that's never a bad thing.

## They Just Might not Remember

*25 September 2010*

When interviewing that relative, keep in mind that there just might be some things they either do not know, never knew, or just cannot remember. It happens to all of us occasionally. Sometimes it is easier to just say "I don't know" when asked for a name or a piece of information. And sometimes it's the truth.

## Re-Evaluate

*27 September 2010*

When was the last time you took a hard look at some conclusions and research you did in the early days of your family history adventure? Any chance you made a mistake?

## Those with No Descendants Might Not Be Listed

*29 September 2010*

Keep in mind that in the cases of intestate estates (where someone died without a valid will), a court usually is not concerned about relatives who die young, never marry, and do not leave any issue. If John dies without children and had six siblings, the court might only list those four siblings of John's who left heirs of their own. The court is concerned with determining heirship—not with compiling a complete genealogy. It all goes back to the original purpose of the record being used.

## Just A Deed?

*30 September 2010*

If you think there should be an estate settlement for an ancestor, make certain to look for a deed even if court records are located. In some cases, there may be no probate and the only record might be a quit claim deed where the heirs transfer property to one of their siblings after the death of the surviving parent. There might not have been any need for an estate settlement. Sometimes our ancestors actually try to avoid going to court.

## Read Carefully

*01 October 2010*

I recently took another look at some pension papers on a relative. Her children were listed, including my great-grandmother. Their great-grandma was listed with a middle name I had never seen anywhere else—not even on her birth certificate. For some reason, it had never "clicked" before that the name was different. I thought I had read the complete list of children with middle names too quickly the first time. The only middle name she ever used was Iona, but there on the pension application for her mother was "Fannie May." Or so I thought. I was confused. It actually said "Fannie May 16 1880," and the "May" was referring to her date of birth. Be careful before jumping to a conclusion and getting a little too excited about locating something "new."

## Adoption or Guardianship?

*02 October 2010*

Adoption records are usually closed and access is often restricted by state law. Is there a chance there was a guardianship for the child instead? Records of guardianships are open and may answer your question. The difficulty is that guardianships are usually for children who have inherited some type of estate—usually through a biological parent. If your "adopted" ancestor was poor, there's less chance of a guardianship.

## Compare to the Census Neighbors

*03 October 2010*

In 1850 and after census records, have you compared your ancestor to his neighbors? Were they from the same place, about the same age, had similar occupations, etc.? Or was your ancestor significantly different from his or her neighbors? It might be a clue.

## Do You Know What It Meant THEN?

*04 October 2010*

Today is 10-4. In CB lingo that means "OK" or something pretty close to that. Is there a phrase or word in a document, letter, or record that meant something different when it was written? Is there a chance you are interpreting something with a 21st century mind when it was written with a 17th century mind?

## Do They Know Their Stuff?

*05 October 2010*

Many of us post genealogical questions on message boards, mailing lists, Facebook groups, etc. Keep in mind that the person who answers may not really "know their stuff," even if they throw around key phrases and sound really smart. Give a second thought before taking free advice or suggestions from someone whose skill level and expertise are not really known to you.

## Think "What Might Have Been Created"

*06 October 2010*

It is always advisable to think of all the records that might have been created when one record is missing. Perhaps the records of your ancestor's estate settlement cannot be found. Are there other court records (perhaps a partition suit) that might have been created? Were there guardianship records for the children? Were there deeds that might have settled up property? Would tax records provide any clues? It can be frustrating when a record is missing, but ask yourself, "what else could there be?

## Chronological Maps

*07 October 2010*

Chronologies are a good problem-solving tool. So are maps. I've got one extended family I'm stuck on and I think that maps of each person's location in certain years (say 1850, 1860, and 1870) might be another helpful tool. Seeing what is "pulling" and "pushing" people to certain locations might be easier if I organize the information in this fashion.

## How Was That First Name Said?

*09 October 2010*

I've been working on Aunt Emma recently. In searching for her in various census records, I have become convinced she pronounced her first name as "Emmer." At least that's how almost every census taker spelled it, Emmar, Emmer, Emer, etc. Think about how the first name was said. Sometime English language names were said in ways that resulted in a wide variety of spellings. *Update*: My aunt's Civil War widow's pension application contained an affidavit regarding her first name. She stated it was "Emmar." Question answered.

## 1910 Census Asks Length of Marriage

*10 October 2010*

Don't forget that the 1910 US Census asked for the length of the current marriage. This can be helpful in estimating a marriage date, and in some cases there will be a notation as to how many times the person has been married. Census takers did not necessarily ask these questions consistently and there is always the possibility your relative did not entirely understand the question.

## Census Questions?

*11 October 2010*

Need to know what questions were asked in what census? Here's a page that has links to all census questions asked in every census from 1850 and onwards: usa.ipums.org/usa/voliii/tEnumForm.shtml

## Don't Forget Half-Siblings

*12 October 2010*

If your ancestor has half siblings, don't forget to search for them as well. In some families, the two sets of children barely interact with their half-siblings. In others, they are as close as full siblings. Just because in one family those relationships were strained doesn't mean they were in others. And your ancestor may have half-siblings and you may not even know it.

## Spelling a Clue to Pronunciation?

*13 October 2010*

Is the spelling of your ancestor's name in a census or other record a clue as to how your relatives said your ancestor's name? Elecksander was probably actually Alexander, said so as to be spelled another way. Cathren in a census was probably Catherine, but probably pronounced "cath rin" as opposed to "Cath er in." Spelling might hide more clues than you think.

## Copyrighting a Fact

*14 October 2010*

As a reminder, facts cannot be copyrighted. The paragraph you write about how you proved a date of birth is something you can copyright and is typically copyrighted the minute you publish it in some form. The fact that Johann was born on 18 June 1832 is not something you can copyright. If facts could be copyrighted, I'd be taking claim to "2 plus 2 equals 4!"

## Chart Everything

*15 October 2010*

I've been working on a relative who was married at least 6 times. To help keep myself organized, I made charts for:

- her marriages,
- where she was in each census year,
- what each census enumeration said about her,
- what years she had what last names,
- who was the father of which children.

Just organizing the information about her helped me keep everything straight in my own mind.

## Watch those Abbreviations

*17 October 2010*

Remember that an abbreviation might not stand for what you think it does. There was a time when "Ia" stood for the state of Indiana, not the state of Iowa as it does today. Make certain you know what something really stands for in the time it was used and not just what it means today.

## Is That First Name Really a Middle Name?

*18 October 2010*

Is what you think is your ancestor's "first name" in reality his or her "middle name? " Your ancestor is simply hiding under a first name that you do not know is his. My Ira Sargent was actually William Ira Sargent and it's as William Sargent that he married in 1870. From 1880 and on he only used the name Ira and was referred to as Ira by his family and never William.

## Don't Just Click, Look Quick, and Go Back

*19 October 2010*

If you've used an online index to take you directly to a record, don't just look at the desired entry and immediately go back to do more searching. Look at the entries before and after the one for your ancestor so you view the document in context and see how it differs from other entries, how it's the same, etc. Make certain you have the entire record as indexes may just lead you to the first page, some sort of reference page, etc.

## Check for Completeness

*20 October 2010*

In any index, be it printed or online, determine how complete it actually is. Are there areas or time periods missing, either because the index or database is in progress or records have been destroyed?

## Scratch it out on Paper

*21 October 2010*

I'm not a big fan of rushing to the computer to enter everything into a database the minute I discover it. Without getting on that soapbox, consider sketching out family relationships on paper before entering them into your genealogical database. Think about the information before you just start mindlessly entering it into a database. Thinking and analyzing are always good. Your initial conclusion may not be the correct one.

## Get Someone Else to Read It

*22 October 2010*

Sometimes another set of eyes will interpret a word, number, or a phrase in a way that simply does not "dawn" on you and may be why additional information seemingly does not make sense or looks to be inconsistent. This can be particularly helpful when an interpretation was done early in your research and has gotten stuck in your head. Those early, incorrect readings of documents can be some of the ones that cause us the most trouble as it is easy to not question them because we've "had it in our head that way for so long."

## Was it Really Their Name?

*24 October 2010*

My great-great-grandmother was Nancy Jane Newman. She was born in 1846 in Indiana to Baptist parents, so there's no birth or christening record. Her life is well-documented (there's no missing years, etc.) and every document shows her as Nancy or Nancy Jane. A lady told me that Nancy was *always* the nickname for Ann and that her *real* name *was* Ann and not Nancy. There are two tips in this: (1) sometimes "nicknames" are not nicknames, and (2) don't listen to anyone who insists that something *always* means something. There are exceptions to everything. Actually, there's a third tip: don't believe everything someone voluntary sends you online either.

## Have You Overlooked an Alternate Spelling?

*25 October 2010*

Is it possible you've overlooked an alternate spelling of a last name? A relative's mother's maiden name was listed in all documents as Morris. Her Social Security Application listed the last name as Morse, which for some strange reason had not crossed my mind. It happens to all of us. Unexpected alternate spellings can be particularly troublesome in families that we've not researched very often or are of an ethnic group with which we are not familiar.

## Leave the Kids Behind?

*26 October 2010*

If your ancestors moved several times, did they leave some children behind, either because the children married or because they died?

One ancestor who moved from Michigan to Iowa and then to Missouri left grown children in Michigan and Iowa, in addition to the children who were with him in Missouri. Remember that the entire family might not have moved with the ancestor. Children who were "of age" might very well have stayed behind.

## Is It a Coincidence?

*27 October 2010*

When I was stuck on my Ira Sargent, there were two families I focused on as being his family of origin. I was "certain" he fit into one of them. Both families had several members named Ira—there had to be one that was "missing." Both families had the same general migration pattern, the age was consistent, etc. Turns out my Ira didn't belong to either one of them, and his family of origin really didn't live where he settled at all. It was his stepfather who, after Ira's mother died, moved the family to where Ira first "appeared." The "other" families may be related, but so distantly that there were likely no real connection. Sometimes similar names and places are coincidences. Just keep that in mind.

## Name Not Changed at Marriage

*28 October 2010*

A relative whose maiden name was Mattie Huls married in the 1890s to a man named George Huls. She signed some legal documents after her marriage related to her mother's estate, but since her name didn't change, I did not immediately realize she was married. Mattie had no descendants and that, combined with her last name never changing, is what nearly caused me to overlook her marriage.

## Start from Scratch

*29 October 2010*

Stuck? Put aside everything you have on an ancestor and "recollect" your information on him.  I'm not saying throw documents and records out. Just think carefully about every assumption you have made and every step in your logic and reasoning and whether each document is really for the "right person" and what it tells you and what it does not. Perhaps starting over is what you need to do to get over that brick wall.

## Secondary Isn't All Bad

*01 November 2010*

Remember, secondary information isn't necessarily wrong. In 1907 a widow testified as to who the siblings of her husband were. Did she know they were her husband's siblings because she had first-hand knowledge of their parentage? No. She did not meet her husband's family until she was in her early teens. She had been told who her husband's siblings were. Did she have reason to doubt it? Probably not. Was she wrong? In this case, that's not likely. She was suing her husband's family over her inheritance and the chance that one of her husband's siblings was left out is fairly slim. It's not 100% proof she was right, but any source needs to be kept in context. She's providing secondary information about the relationship because she was not present at the births of her husband's siblings. That doesn't mean she's incorrect. Given that she was involved in a court case with her husband's siblings in the area where they all were from, the chance that she lied or left one out is minimal.

Note: Since this court case was over an inheritance, the court would only have been concerned about living heirs of the deceased husband. Siblings who died without issue would not need to be mentioned.

# Is the Line Down the Middle?

*02 November 2010*

My brother lives in a rural area a mile or so from my parents on the same state highway. He lives on the east side of the road. They are on the west. The township line runs right on the road—consequently, they live in different townships. Is it possible that your "near neighbor" ancestors live in different townships or counties, etc.? That would impact where certain records are kept and stored. Think about where the lines are located in relation to where your family lived. Near neighbors may never appear in records as neighbors if the lines are in the right place.

# Read the Little Handwriting

*03 November 2010*

Are there two lines of handwritten script squeezed in the bottom of Grandma's marriage record? Is there something written in the margin of the deed book? If the clerk or officer of the court took the time and effort to "squeeze it in," then there's probably a reason for it. It may be a "boring legal reason" or it may be a significant clue. Even "boring legal reasons" may have research consequences. Find out what it says and what it means.

# Directories Can Fill in Missing Years

*04 November 2010*

If you have urban ancestors (or even not-so-urban ones), consider using city directories to fill in those off-census years. Directories may list others in the household (particularly if they are old enough to be employed, but still living at home) and can document moves in off-census years. Directories can also help you find people in the census when the indexes fail. Always copy the page with the abbreviations that is often at the front of the reference. They are fairly standard, but many books have a few abbreviations that are somewhat localized.

## Is It Just a Little Typo That's Confusing You?

*05 November 2010*

Sometimes one letter can make a big difference and move a location across the country. I was typing an address and I intended to type "CA" for California. Instead I typed "VA" and implied Virginia. I corrected the error, but it would have been easy to create confusion—after all, it is a state abbreviation. Keokuk County, Iowa, could easily become Keokuk, Iowa, with the drop of the word "County." Sometimes typographical errors or errors of omission are obvious and sometimes they are not.

## Are You Their Only Descendant?

*06 November 2010*

If you are looking for information or ephemera related to your great-great-grandparents, ask yourself: "Am I their descendant?" Chances are you are not and any other descendant could have information or materials. It's not often that one person is the only descendant of a given set of great-great-grandparents.

## Did the Middle Initial Get Merged?

*07 November 2010*

Is your ancestor's name David P. Able? Is it possible in a record somewhere that he is listed as David Pable? Depending upon the handwriting, the letters, and other factors, a middle initial can sometimes be read as part of the last or even the first name.

## You Are Not Your Great-Grandma

*08 November 2010*

Sometimes we might have an idea of what great-grandma or great-grandpa did in response to a certain event in their lives. Be careful assuming that you know exactly what great-grandma or great-grandpa would have done. Sometimes you may very well be right. Stick to what you really know and don't tell others that you know how a long-deceased relative would act. You don't. Thinking you know what you don't can create additional research frustrations.

## You Can't Break Every Brick Wall Online

*09 November 2010*

Some genealogists think if they post their question to enough message boards, websites, mailing lists, and Facebook groups, someone will discover that magic missing piece and share it with them. That is not the way it works. Remember that not every problem can be solved completely by getting help online. The answer to your problem might lie in a document or a record in a courthouse that has never been digitized. Asking for online help is always a good idea, especially when you are unfamiliar with the time period, location, records, etc. Online communication can provide you with insight into records and how they are accessed, but not every problem can be solved completely by posting online.

## Are the Records Public or Not?

*10 November 2010*

It is important to remember that some records we use in our genealogy research are not public records and may only be available to us through the courtesy of the record holder. Funeral homes, businesses, and churches do not have to allow genealogists to use their records. It does not matter how much money your great-great-grandma gave to the diocese or paid for their funeral. Many do allow access, but these organizations are different from local or state governments that maintain records. Government records are open and subject to a variety of restrictions. Private business records are private and genealogy research is not usually a reason to get a search warrant or a subpoena.

# US Draft Registrations and Classification Records

*11 November 2010*

US records of Selective Service registrations (aka draft registrations) for men born before January 1st, 1960 are available through the National Archives. For more information on access and cost, visit www.archives.gov/st-louis/selective-service. This site also has information on obtaining copies of classification records for registrants (for draftees and non-draftees) as well. *FamilySearch* has World War I and World War II draft registrations available online. *Ancestry.com* also has Civil War draft registrations available on their site.

# Multiple Tombstone Transcriptions

*12 November 2010*

If the tombstone of great-great-grandpa is difficult to read today, have you searched to see if the cemetery's stones were transcribed twenty years ago, thirty years ago, or earlier? Perhaps the stone was much easier to read in 1960 than it is today and perhaps someone transcribed it.

# Is That Administrator Really Unrelated?

*14 November 2010*

Your ancestor's estate is being administrated by a man whose name you have never heard. Any chance he is the son-in-law? If the deceased had no children, any chance he is the husband of a niece?

# Cousins with the Same Name

*15 November 2010*

In some areas, it's important to remember that the reason there may be several men with the same name of about the same age is that they are all named for their paternal grandfather. If Henry Puffer has four sons and they all name a son Henry, and they remain in the area, that's four Henry Puffers to sort out.

## Fire Insurance Maps

*16 November 2010*

Fire insurance maps may provide you with a different view of where your ancestor lived. Insurance maps are generally available between the late 19<sup>th</sup> and early 20<sup>th</sup> centuries for United States cities large and small. These maps may tell you what type of home your ancestor lived in, the type of construction it was, how many stories it was, etc. The maps showing neighboring homes may also provide an idea of the "feel" of the neighborhood (did they have large lots, were they crammed together, etc.). Nearby churches and schools may be identified as well. The Library of Congress website has more information at www.loc.gov/collections/sanborn-maps and searches at Worldcat (www.worldcat.org) for "sanborn map yourtown" may locate some references as well. It is possible that your local library has digital access to these maps for the state in which the library is located.

## *Et al.* and *Et ux.*

*17 November 2010*

These Latin abbreviations are found in many legal documents, particularly land records and court cases. "*Et al.*" means "and others," indicating that multiple individuals were selling property, buying property, suing someone, or being sued. "*Et ux.*" means "and spouse" and that your ancestor and their spouse were selling property, buying property, suing, or being sued. In some cases, *et al.* will be used when the "other" is a spouse. Whenever a group of people are involved in a court case or a land record, it has higher potential to provide genealogically relevant information as inheritances or partial ownership interests are often involved.

# Getting Confused?

*18 November 2010*

Remember that family members can easily mix up deceased relatives, resulting in more confusion for the researcher. An ancestor's wife's name was Ellen, and the family was full of stories about Ellen and her life. The ancestor's sister was Emma. The more I learn about Emma, the more I realize that some of the stories that were told about Ellen were actually about Emma. It is easy to see how one could get the names mixed up, particularly if they had never met either person. The names do not have to be remotely similar for someone to confuse them or to merge them into one individual. Is it possible that what grandma told you about relative A was actually about relative B?

## A Child's Memory of Partial Details

*19 November 2010*

Is Grandma telling you information about events that took place when she was a child? Sometimes children get things correct and sometimes they don't. This situation can be aggravated if the adults don't really tell the child anything and the child only overhears a few details and creates a story in their head to fit them. Sometimes they, without any ill intent, create details to fit what they hear, or they interpret things through a child's eyes, which may not be entirely correct. That story, having resided in their head for so long, becomes fact. If you have children of your own, think about how they misunderstood something once in a while. Then remember: Grandma was a child once, too!

## Could It Have Triggered a Newspaper Writeup?

*20 November 2010*

Think about the various events in your ancestor's life that were noteworthy. People often look for births, marriages, and deaths in the newspaper. Most people think to look for criminal activity to be mentioned as well. But that's not all. Are there other events in their life that might have warranted attention? One ancestor had a special examiner from the pension office come to her rural town to interview her and five relatives in 1902. It took two days to complete the testimony. Any chance that might have been mentioned in the "gossip column" that week? Possibly. Think about other non-vital events that might have been written up in the local newspaper.

## What Is a Life Estate?

*21 November 2010*

If a legal document indicates your ancestor has a "life estate," in real estate it means they own it for their life only. They can't sell it or mortgage it and they can't bequeath it, either. They have it as long as they have "life," and as long as they pay taxes. But astute readers already knew they couldn't avoid taxes!

## Enumerated Twice?

*22 November 2010*

It is always possible that your ancestor is enumerated more than once in a census year, which we have discussed before. Marital discord is another reason why someone may be enumerated twice: at home, supposedly living with his family, and again in a rental property or boarding house of some type. The wife may not have wanted neighbors to know that the husband didn't really live there, so she told the census taker that he did. When the landlord, boarding house owner, etc. reported him as well, he ended up being listed twice.

*John Henry Ufkes (1917-2003)*

*taken near Basco, Hancock County, Illinois*

# Chapter 14: Merging Saints, Circle Searching, Flukes, and Running Home

## Widowed or Not?

*23 November 2010*

Marital status as stated in some records needs to be taken with a grain of salt. Back in the day when divorce was scandalous, a person enumerated in a census as "widowed" might actually have been divorced. I never searched for a divorce record for a relative as the husband left the area (unknown to me) and the marital status of the wife simply was widowed from that time on. This was in a location that did not have civil registration of deaths and had simply concluded he died with no record of it being created.

## Drop the H?

*24 November 2010*

I'm searching for a man named Harm Habbus. One suggestion in searching for him was to search for the last name of Abbus. An initial "H" is one of those letters that can get left off a name, depending upon how it is pronounced and heard. Most sites that support Soundex searches ignore the letter "h," but only if it is NOT the first letter. Could your "H" people be hiding without their "H?" Hartman could be Artman, etc.

## Merging a Saint

*25 November 2010*

Is your ancestor's last name St. Clair or some other phrase starting with the word "Saint?" Is it possible that the "saint" was merged into the rest of the name, resulting in Sinclair or a similar rendering? Is it possible your ancestor's middle and last names merged into one? Sometimes when I tell people my name is

Michael Neill, they think I am saying "Mike O'Neill." Did something similar happen with your ancestor's name?

## Will Locals Research at the Courthouse?

*26 November 2010*

If onsite research at the local courthouse is not an option, consider contacting the local genealogical/historical society or the local library. They may be able to give you names of researchers, have suggestions for doing research remotely, or may be able to do some limited research for you via mail. Not every courthouse responds to a mail inquiry and those that do may not search all the variants in the way they need to be searched. It all depends on how diligent the clerk or their assistant is and how willing they are to search the records for a non-tax paying, out-of-area resident.

## Put Everything in Context

*27 November 2010*

Put every event in context. If your ancestor sells property, ask yourself:

- How old was he?
- Was he getting ready to leave the area?
- Was he having financial problems?
- Was he selling to a child or other relative?
- Did he buy other property about the same time?

Don't look at a record all by itself. Put it in the context of other things that were taking place in your ancestor's life.

## Searching in Circles?

*28 November 2010*

I usually tell researchers if they spend more than five minutes searching for a person in an online database, it's time to get off the computer and organize their search procedure. The first step is to determine if it would be more efficient to search the database manually, especially if certain details about the family are known that would make manual searching easier. If manual searching isn't going to work, make a chart and organize your searches by how you will be entering the search terms. Think about:

- first name
- middle names
- last name
- spelling variants
- birthdate
- place of birth
- other search parameters

Chart up how you will perform your searches and do them systematically. You might be surprised at the results. The chart can also serve as a research log.

## Leave Out the Last Name

*30 November 2010*

When searching an online database, leave out the last name and enter in other search parameters. Is it possible that the last name was so difficult to read on the original record that it was simply omitted when the information was transcribed? Did it get transcribed in a way that means no amount of permutations with crazy spelling and wildcard searches will locate it? If you enter a last name as a search term, it will have to be in the database in order for the entry to be returned as a "hit." Try going without.

## Abbreviated the First Names

*01 December 2010*

Is it possible that in the census or other record your relatives' names have been abbreviated, or that only initials have been used? Census takers, writers of passenger lists, and others would occasionally use just initials. Saves on spelling, saves time, saves ink, but increases frustration for researchers.

## Vowel and Consonant Interchanged?

*02 December 2010*

It's easy for most researchers to realize that vowels can easily get interchanged in a name, resulting in variant spellings (eg. Trautvetter and Troutvetter). Soundex searches ignore vowels in an attempt to get around this problem. Remember that consonants and vowels can get interchanged in names as well, particularly if the handwriting is not all that great. These variations can be particularly troublesome until the researcher realizes the problem. Trautvetter often gets transcribed as "Trantvetter," when the "u" is read as an "n." The sound of the name has changed significantly, and a Soundex-based search for Trautvetter will not locate Trantvetter. Are vowel and consonant interchanges causing your problems when doing searches?

## Is It Worth the Time to Find It?

*03 December 2010*

Are you spending too much time looking for a specific record that really might not even help your research all that much? There's a couple for whom I cannot find their mid-1800 passenger list entry when they arrived in the United States. I've charted out my search attempts to make certain I have looked for all reasonable spellings and have searched for variants of the parents' names as well as the names of the children who immigrated with them.

After some thought, I'm not really certain I need it—at least not bad enough to spend an inordinate amount of time trying to find it. I have a good idea of where the family is from in Europe, as I know where the husband's brother was born. I know what children the couple had and where they settled. The mid-1800 passenger list probably isn't going to tell me where they were from (although it is possible). After having spent at least several hours trying to find them, it may be best to work on locating other records on them in the United States. Those records may help me locate their manifest entry. It would be nice to know when they immigrated, but sometimes things cannot be found for one reason or another. It is occasionally necessary to realize that it may be time to work on other things.

## Do You Know What All Those Search Options Do?

*04 December 2010*

When using a search option at an online database, do you know how that site implements wildcard searches, Soundex searches, and other search options? Getting creative with search terms is often necessary, but if you don't know how they are really working, you are not being effective. Experiment and look at your results and see if you are getting what you think you should. A Soundex search for the last name Smut on a site with English language last names should result in a large number of hits. And if you don't know why, then review what Soundex really is.

## Are You Reading and Paying Attention?

*06 December 2010*

Are you really reading, thinking about, and interpreting the information you have found? Or are your eyes merely passing over the words, looking for that obvious clue? Sometimes the biggest clues are not all that obvious. It's easy to catch the low-hanging fruit of explicit statements and blatant clues. Go back and re-read and think about what a document says. Are there clues you bypassed the first time you "sped read" that record?

## Unusual Combinations May Just Be A Fluke

*08 December 2010*

Don't assume that just because the names are "close" to the ones you are looking for that they have to be a match. I was looking for information on a William Bell who married a Martha Sargent in Iowa in the later part of the 19<sup>th</sup> century. Turns out there was another William Bell in the same part of Iowa who married a Lorinda Sargent. Two totally separate couples from two separate families. This determination was made by research, not just guessing that they weren't related. How many William Bells can marry a Sargent and live a few counties away from each other? Apparently two. Two distinct ones. It can happen. Don't force people to be related.

## Local Library

*09 December 2010*

Have you contacted the local library in the town/county where your ancestors lived? Is it possible they have access to resources that aren't available elsewhere or aren't online? Or do they know of any unique suggestions for research in their local area? Do they know of any local genealogists who are experts in materials in their area and familiar with local families as well?

## Where They Knew No One

*10 December 2010*

We often suggest to researchers that people move in groups and settle where they know someone. Most of the time, people do. Keep in mind, however, that once in a while people move where they know absolutely no one. One ancestral couple could not be located. They simply evaporated. They were not near any of their children, any of his siblings, or any of her siblings. They migrated to an area of Missouri where no one they knew lived. Sometimes it does happen. Sometimes when it happens and we think there's "no reason" for the move, there actually was, but it is a reason that we have yet to discover and potentially one for which there is no extant record.

## Grandma's Not Primary for Her Birth Information

*11 December 2010*

Remember that Grandma is not considered someone who can provide primary information about her own date and place of birth. It's not that she is wrong, but that most people are not typically considered to be firsthand witnesses of their own birth.

## First Name Translations

*12 December 2010*

Keep in mind that if your ancestor translated his or her name, they might have used conventional translations others from their ethnic area used or they might have made up their own. Some non-English names had common translations (Jans and Johann becoming John or Wilhelm, and Willm becoming William) and others did not (the Greek Panagiotis and the low-German Heye). Some translations are easy to understand, such as Hinrich becoming Henry. Jacobus being the Latin form of James is one that some people recognize immediately and others may not.

The question that should be in your mind is: if my immigrant ancestor has an English name, do I know what that could have been in his original language? What other names sound similar to that name as well (because not every person translated their name directly)? Is it possible that my non-English speaking ancestor actually had an English name to begin with?

## Did They Run Back Home?

*13 December 2010*

While tracking a relative through census records, it appears that she left Missouri shortly before her first marriage, moved to Oklahoma, and stayed. Forty years later, after a divorce, she appears in that original Missouri county in one census record. If I had not known where her family was from, her residence there would have seemed pretty random. Now I'm reminded that occasionally when a residence seems random that there might just be something I don't know.

## Same Name Does Not Mean Same Person

*14 December 2010*

It does not matter how odd the name is, it doesn't have to be the same person if the name's the same. A distant relative of mine claimed that my aunt died in Chicago in 1935, because he found someone with her same name dying there. The problem is that the Chicago person isn't my relative. If he had done research in the local records where the family actually lived (two hundred miles from Chicago), he would have located the person's probate file, which indicated she died in the 1950s. Just because the name's the same doesn't mean the person is. When in doubt, check it out.

A two-pronged approach could have solved this problem. Search for my aunt and the 1935 death in all US census records when they were alive. The 1910, 1920, and 1930 census would have easily solved this problem as both women with this unusual name were alive in those years and enumerated: one in Chicago and my aunt, downstate.

## Heir Versus Legatee

*17 December 2010*

While state statute usually defines these terms, it is generally true that an heir (often referred to as an "heir-at-law") of a deceased person is someone who inherits from the deceased based upon their biological relationship to the deceased and state statute's definition of who qualifies as an heir. The heirs-at-law of a deceased individual are those who have an inheritance interest in the estate. Spouse and children are the typical heirs-at-law. Depending upon the family structure and what other relatives are also dead, it can include cousins, siblings, nephews, etc. A legatee is usually someone mentioned in the will of a deceased person. A legatee can also be an heir-at-law but doesn't have to be. Heirs are related. Legatees may be related, but they don't have to be.

## Do You Have the Correct Database?

*22 December 2010*

Always make certain you know what you are searching. I recently wasted fifteen minutes searching for someone in the 1900 census, before I realized the database I was actually querying was the 1930 census.

## Did They Cross the Wrong Letter?

*23 December 2010*

If your ancestor's last name has a "t" in it, did the cross on the "t" cover another letter and "change" the name? My Butlers became Butters for that very reason.

## Name Split in the Wrong Place?

*24 December 2010*

The man's name was Mel Verslius. His World War 2 draft card accidentally listed him as Melver Sluis before they made the correction. Any chance your ancestor's name "got split" in the wrong place?

## Track the "Whys" of Your Research

*25 December 2010*

It is important somewhere to keep track of your research logic as you progress. You might not remember why you are researching a certain person, especially if it is a somewhat distant collateral relative. While at the Allen County Public Library last August, I focused on a certain Benjamin Butler in 1850 as being "mine." Using that enumeration as the starting point, I searched other records and made research progress. A stack of papers and records. One problem—I didn't track why I thought this 1850 census entry was for the correct person, as the entry was not an obvious match to what I knew about my Benjamin. It took me hours to reconstruct my reasoning. When I decided the 1850 guy was "mine," I should have written down my reasons. That would have saved time and allowed me to later determine if my reasoning was still sound.

## One Wrong Letter Makes a Difference

*26 December 2010*

A record stated that a relative was born in Fort Huron. The actual location was Port Huron. One letter can make a difference.

## Is Each Piece of Paper for the Same Person?

*29 December 2010*

When locating records and putting them in your files, make certain that just because the "name's the same" that you actually have the same person. Make certain age, location, implied social status, and other information "match" or are reasonably consistent. If you are not reasonably certain, keep the information, but don't attach it to your person and alter what you know about him to make all the records "fit." It may require a bit of sorting out if continued research suggests that you've merged two different individuals together.

## Read a Book

*31 December 2010*

I have been reading *First Generations: Women in Colonial America* for the past several days. It has given me some insight into the colonial experience of women and caused me to think about a few things in ways I never have. Is there a history text or sociological study that might expand your knowledge, even if it doesn't directly expand your family tree?

## Citing the Source

*01 January 2011*

Genealogy software programs can help genealogists cite their source, but sometimes they have limitations. Whole books, such as *Evidence Explained*, have been written providing guidelines for tracking where information was located. Remember that if nothing else, a citation should provide enough detail to get you back to the page in a book, piece of paper, or website (if it's still around later) that provided you some information. If it doesn't, it's probably not adequate. A relative said, "a newspaper in 1909 mentioned" a family member. At the very least, the name of the paper, date of publication, and whether it was the print, microfilm, or digital version would have been helpful. Page number and section, if appropriate, would also make locating the item easier. It's not always necessary to be 100% correct in the form of your citation, but it should allow someone else to re-find what you found—even if that "someone else" is you. The form in which you found it (original book or manuscript/record, microfilm, digital, etc.) help you know how "far" from the "original" what you viewed was. After all, once in a while we need to review things for an additional viewing.

Don't let bad memories of footnotes in a former English class scare you away from citation. For most genealogists, it does not make a whit of difference where you put the comma, semicolon, etc. Just get the essence of how and where you got that document.

## How Precise Is that Relationship?

*02 January 2011*

If Aunt Margaret tells you someone is her "cousin," what does she really mean? First cousin, second cousin, etc.? To the genealogist, it makes a difference. First cousins (who share grandparents) are different from second cousins (who share great-grandparents). First cousins once removed are of different generations from the common ancestor—the grandparent of one was the great-grandparent of another. It's not necessary to confuse Aunt Margaret with these distinctions. Instead of getting her to tell you the precise word, have her explain the way they were related, generation by generation, or ask her about how they were related (your mothers were sisters, your dad and her mom were brother and sister, etc.). You can figure out the precise word for the relationship later, and asking those questions to clarify the relationship may elicit more information anyway!

## Purpose of the Record

*05 January 2011*

Remember the purpose of the record when analyzing the information it contains. A birth certificate really is about the birth, and minor errors in where the mother was born (if the certificate even contains that information) might not have been considered material. A probate judge was concerned that a person was dead and that probate proceedings should start and might not be overly worried about the person's precise date of death. A census was to count people and provide other certain statistical information for the government. The enumerator might not have been overly concerned if occasionally he confused a few children with stepchildren.

## Pick Out Every Date

*06 January 2011*

Sometimes when I'm stuck in analyzing a document or an entire record, especially one that is lengthy and may mention several events or dates, I pick out every date and put those events in a chronology. I look also at statements that don't mention a "specific date" and ask myself if those statements suggest a date or time frame.

This can take some time if the record in question is a lengthy, drawn-out court case, but it can help you to understand the legal maneuverings in order to determine what's significant and what is not. You might be surprised at what you realize you have overlooked.

*chronology created from a widow's pension affidavit*

| Year | Event |
| --- | --- |
| About 1795 | Harrison Ramsey born. |
| Before Mexican War | Harrison Ramsey's first wife (unnamed) died. |
| 1846 | Harrison and Andrew Ramsey work in the Galena, Illinois, mines. |
| 1847 | Harrison and Andrew Ramsey enlist in Mexican War. |
| During Mexican War | Andrew Ramsey died. |
| 1854 | Harrison Ramsey meets Eliza Jane. |
| 1855 | Harrison Ramsey marries Eliza Jane. |
| 1858 | Harrison Ramsey dies. |
| 1892 | Eliza Jane Ramsey makes out an affidavit in support of her widow's pension claim. |

# Are the Witnesses Just Neighbors?

*08 January 2011*

When genealogists look at their ancestor's will, they usually pay attention to the witnesses. They should as those names can be clues. However, witnesses are not necessarily related to the deceased. They may simply be neighbors. An ancestor wrote her will in 1902. The witnesses were not relatives. When I looked them up in the 1900 census, the ancestor who wrote the will and the two witnesses were all enumerated on the same census page. Witnesses just legally have to be warm bodies of legal age who saw the person sign the document. One thing about witnesses to a will—the witness should not be named in the will or benefit from it. That's usually considered a conflict.

## Watch the Genders on Those Foreign Language Names and Records

*11 January 2011*

Are you making certain you have the right gender for the ancestor in that baptismal record? A researcher connected a baptismal record to her one ancestor. One problem: the name on the record is a male name in the language in which the records are written and the record also clearly uses the word for son and not daughter. If you don't know the language and the record does not indicate gender (make certain the entire record entry has been read), find out the usual gender of someone with that name. The ability to recognize names will come with time and practice. Make certain you are getting gender advice from someone familiar with the actual language and dialect your family spoke. It may be helpful to create a master list with names and the typical gender for those names, otherwise the mess you end up making could partially be your own fault.

## Was He Missed by the Census Taker?

*12 January 2011*

It is possible that your ancestor was missed by the census taker, but make certain you have truly searched adequately first, including a manual page-by-page search if necessary and practical. It is possible, unbeknownst to you, that your ancestor lived somewhere else for a very short time and a distance from the expected residence. People also occasionally get overlooked by the census taker, especially if they move around a lot or otherwise live a lifestyle that puts them at risk for being overlooked.

## What Were They Smokin' When They Gave That Information?

*14 January 2011*

Let's face it, sometimes information on a document is flat out incorrect. It may be that the ancestor lied, someone misunderstood something, etc. but the fact remains: they lied. Lies may permeate the record, be carefully sprinkled throughout it, or just dropped in one place like a genealogy confusion time bomb waiting to strike. When you think you have a situation like this, organize all your documents and outline your reasons for why you think the one document is wrong and where it is wrong. That will help you make your case and allow others to see if they agree with you. Don't just say "this one fact is wrong." Write up your reasoning and make your case, carefully and clearly, because occasionally what you initially think is wrong is actually correct.

## Are Soundex Searches Right for Your Last Names?

*15 January 2011*

Soundex searches are search approaches available on many online sites. Keep in mind that Soundex generally works best with names of English or Germanic origin. Soundex searches for Neill bring up results of Newell, Neal, Nial, Neel, Nowel, Neil, etc. Some are more reasonable variants than others, but Soundex works fairly well on this last name. There are problems with non-English names when Soundex searches are used. A Soundex search for Robidoux will not locate Robido, a very reasonable variant. French names are a good example of a language where Soundex searches are sometimes weak, but it is not the only language that Soundex is not really geared towards. There are other languages that present similar challenges to Soundex based searches. Is the Soundex search option limiting your search?

## US Passport Applications for Sisters-in-Law

*16 January 2011*

Passport applications for married women in the United States in the early 1900s often included information on the citizenship status and nativity for their husbands or fathers (depending upon the marital status of the applicant). Is there a female whose information on her husband could be helpful to your research? Wives of two uncles applied for passports in the 1920s and gave detailed information on their husbands even though none of them were immigrants to the United States.

It wasn't just women. During this time period, men may also have provided information on their fathers, particularly if the father was born outside the United States.

## Female Obituaries that Never Mention Their Name

*17 January 2011*

Remember that obituaries for women may never mention their name. It may be necessary to search for their husband's name when performing online searches of digital newspapers to locate their obituary. I spent hours searching for the obituary of a Belle Shaw, who died in 1945. I only knew the year of her death and that she died in Ohio. No amount of clever searching based upon her name brought the desired result. Her obituary in the Zanesville, Ohio, newspaper listed her as "Mrs. Louis Shaw." Her first name is never mentioned. Shaw himself had been dead several years by the time his wife died and I had initially not searched for his name much past his date of death. That was a mistake.

## Court Those Newspapers

*18 January 2011*

If your ancestor was involved in some type of "sensational" court case, check out the newspapers around the time the case was heard in court. Review the actual court records to determine the dates or terms of court when the court acted on the case. A local newspaper may mention the case and provide details not listed in the actual court records during those times when the case was on the current court docket. Of course, newspapers don't always get all the facts right, but there still may be nuggets of information in the papers that do not appear in the actual court record.

## They Didn't Always Require Paperwork

*20 January 2011*

Wonder why great-great-grandma's age changes so much from one record to another? One reason could be that she wanted to shave a few years off her age. Life was also different when great-great-grandma was providing information in the late 1800s. She might not have been concerned that if her age didn't match in various records that she would have a problem with her pension, passport, insurance, credit bureau file, and other records. Life was in some ways very different in 1880 than it is today.

And great-great-grandma probably didn't have to provide any evidence for those ages she provided in those records. That makes a difference as well.

## Is the Original Unclear and Easy to Misinterpret?

*21 January 2011*

I've changed the names and location, but here is part of a birth announcement I read recently: "...paternal grandparents are Jim and Lori Smith of Dingdongtown. Paternal great-grandparents are Susan Smith, Plowville, and the late Bubba Smith and Ken and Susan Markle of Allentown." The question is: are Ken and Susan alive or dead? People living today know what the paper intended. What would someone in fifty years think?

## Image Copy, Transcription, Extract?

*22 January 2011*

When you are obtaining a copy of a document or record, are you getting an image copy (which usually means a printed digital reproduction or a photocopy), a transcription (which usually means someone hand copied or typed up the whole document), or an extract (which transcribes relevant parts of the document)? The three obviously are not the same. If you have an extract or a transcription and things are not clear, you might want to obtain an image copy if at all possible.

## Naturalization Through the Father

*23 January 2011*

In the United States before until the early part of the 20$^{th}$ century, generally speaking, when a father naturalized, his minor children automatically became citizens as well. This type of citizenship is referred to as derivative. Before 1906, minor children were rarely named in their father's naturalization record, but his naturalization effectively served as their naturalization record. Children who were over twenty-one at the time of their father's naturalization did not become citizens through their father's naturalization. They would typically have to naturalize on their own. This might explain why some individuals have no naturalization records and yet appear as "naturalized" on census and other records. For some this may have eventually been a problem if they were unable to provide proof of when their father naturalized and their own citizenship was called into question. Some of these individuals would naturalize again in their own right just to clarify their status.

## Reading the Name Again

*24 January 2011*

Years ago, a distant relative interpreted the name of a child of an ancestor as "Pine." Decades later, another relative viewed the original record where "Pine" was located and determined that the script did not say "Pine." It actually read "Jane." Pine is still floating around as a first name for this individual in print materials, databases, and websites. Sometimes it pays to go back and doublecheck—even if the original compiler appears to be someone who knows what they are doing.

## Are Three Sources Enough?

*25 January 2011*

There is an old adage in genealogical research that "three sources are proof." Not so. Remember that three "sources" of the same information may actually come from the same source. Think about who likely provided information for the death certificate, the obituary, and the tombstone. They probably were the same person. Try (where possible) to get information from sources that likely had different informants. While that's not always possible (especially in frontier states/time periods and in the American South), three sources agreeing is not magic.

## If the Sources Don't Match

*26 January 2011*

If sources don't match, don't assume that the information they provide is incorrect. If you have two different dates of birth, is it possible there were actually two different people with the same name? There are many reasons records can give differing information. Keep yourself open to the possibility that records you think are for the same person are actually for two different people. Don't force everything to match. There may be two individuals hanging out in the same location at about the same time who are about the same age. They may or may not be related. Don't force that, either. Let the records speak for themselves.

## You May Have to Let It Go

*27 January 2011*

Consider how much time you have spent trying to locate that one record. It might be time to work on something else. I have a relative for whom their life from 1847-1855 is documented in several records: marriage, a land purchase, declaration of intent, 1855 state census, probate, and guardianship for children. I cannot find him in the 1850 census. In this case, it might not be worth it to spend days searching for him in the 1850 census—particularly if I have documented all my search attempts and how those searches were conducted. Of course if something changes (a new index is released, I discover a new variant spelling, my known information about the ancestor or his family structure changes, etc.) then I should look again. Otherwise I might want to focus on other records. Just a thought.

## Is the Title Misleading?

*28 January 2011*

The first time you use a database or website, make certain you know what you are using and understand where the data is from. Titles can be misleading or incomplete. Don't assume it "can't be my person" because the title doesn't make any sense. Actually look at the record and determine what it is. A finding aid I recently used supposedly contained only veterans of the Civil War and later conflicts, yet there was a War of 1812 veteran thrown into the mix.

## One Day of No Research

*29 January 2011*

Consider a day (or two) of no actual research to locate new information. Instead, organize and enter into your database information you have already located. You may even make some discoveries in the process. '

## 1860 Census Marriage Clues

*30 January 2011*

Don't forget that the 1860 US census asks individuals if they were married within the census year—the twelve months before the date of the census, 1 June 1860.

*Stillwell School, 1915,*

*Stillwell, Hancock County, Illinois*

*Connie (Ufkes) Neill, Dorothy (Habben) Ufkes,
and John Henry Ufkes, 1954, taken in Chicago,
Cook County, Illinois*

# Chapter 15: Self-Checking, Boarders, Farmed Out, and Widow Power

## Check Yourself

*31 January 2011*

Years ago, I made an extract from a document and incorrectly typed the year as 1850. I've repeated that year numerous times. I recently retrieved the original document and in reading it realized that the year of the record was actually 1852. As the document is the first one that places the person in his "new location," the year is crucial. Because I corrected myself, I have to go back and re-evaluate some conclusions that hinged upon the 1850 year. It pays to periodically review your own extracts and transcriptions.

## Does That Document Allow You to Estimate Age?

*01 February 2011*

Remember that in order to do certain things such as getting married, writing a will, buying property, or voting, a person had to be a certain age. Is an estimate of your ancestor's age hiding in a document because you didn't make the connection?

## Those Boarders Might be More

*03 February 2011*

Are there one or two boarders with your family in the census? Just because they are listed as a boarder doesn't mean that they aren't related. Boarders could easily be nephews, nieces, or other family members temporarily staying in the household. See if any identifying information in that person's enumeration suggests a connection (place of birth, occupation, etc.). Try to find the boarder in other records to determine if there is a connection to your family. Tracing the boarder could lead you to more information on the ancestor of interest.

## Be Negative and Record It

*04 February 2011*

Are you keeping track of the people who weren't the right ones and why they weren't the correct ones? Often a researcher will run into the same "wrong" people over and over. Tracking them in at least outline form and having that information handy may keep you from researching the same people over and over only to learn you already eliminated them a long time ago. It may be helpful to also create a longer document where you indicate clearly why this person is not the right one. If it ever turns out that they are distantly related, you've already got some of the work done on that person. If you ever have to change what you know about your "right" person, you can re-evaluate the reasons why you thought some people were the wrong ones. That can't be done if you don't keep track.

## Similar Names May be Different People

*05 February 2011*

Just because names are the same does not mean it's one person with a variant name. My ancestor was Nancy Jane Newman. She had a first cousin named Nancy Elizabeth Newman. To further confuse the issue, they married brothers. Researchers frequently confuse them. It can be easy to do, but remember—just because you think the names mean the people are the same doesn't mean they are. Do your research and take care before determining you have the same person with two slightly different names. You may have two very different people with similar names.

## Multiple Records of Same Event

*06 February 2011*

Always keep in mind that there may be multiple records that may provide information on the date of an event. The date of your ancestor's death may be in a county book of death records, an obituary, a church register, a tombstone, the family bible, his pension record, etc. There may be a note that he is deceased in a deed, a tax roll, or a probate journal. Not all these records are equally reliable. Just remember that an event may be recorded in more than one place, and don't neglect to check records despite thinking "I already have that." One never knows what additional information a similar source may provide.

## Does Your Own Handwriting Give You Another Variant?

*07 February 2011*

In reviewing handwritten notes for an article, I looked at the way I had written the last name Butler. If I had not known what the word was, I really might have been inclined to think it was "Beetler." I remember a time when someone told me that they way I wrote my last name made it look like it was "Niece." Maybe if you are not having luck with spelling variants, try writing sloppy and have someone else read it!

## How Old Should They Have Been?

*08 February 2011*

We all know census records can contain incorrect ages. When searching online databases, besides having the years of birth for people I am looking for, I have their approximate age in specific census years on a sheet in front of me. This helps me eyeball if I might or might not have the correct people. Having only the years of birth in front of me is helpful, but having the approximate at the time of the census saves me a little bit of time and reduces errors because I subtracted wrong in my head.

## Grandma Is Human & So Are You

*09 February 2011*

Remember that any relative, even the most well-meaning and reliable one, can occasionally tell you something that is incorrect.

Verify everything Grandma (or Uncle Herman, etc.) tells you, using other sources as much as possible. Well-intentioned informants can be incorrect and the very process of verifying what they tell you may cause you to locate information you never dreamed of. People tell me that "I didn't look at that record because I already knew what was on it because Grandma told me." You don't know what is on that record until you actually look. You may think you know and you may be correct, but there's always the chance that you were wrong.

## Don't Grab the First Match

*10 February 2011*

Remember that there might be more than one person who fits the details of the person for whom you are looking. I was working on a George Butler, born in 1848 in Michigan, the son of a Benjamin Butler. Turns out there were two completely unrelated George Butlers born in Michigan in 1848, sons of Benjamin. To top it off, the Benjamins were both born around 1819 or so in the same state. Look around when you locate a match and make certain there is not another match nearby. You may end up researching the wrong person if you are not careful.

## Middle Names That Are Last Names

*12 February 2011*

Some descendants of Maryland native Thomas Johnson Rampley assumed his middle name was his mother's maiden name. While sometimes middle names that are "last names" are the maiden name of the mother, that is not always the case. The name could have come from a neighbor, another family member, or a famous contemporary person. I'm not certain where it came from in Thomas' case. Middle names that are last names may also be a patronymic name, one based upon the father's first name as in the case of German native Anke Hinrichs Fecht, whose father was Hinrich Fecht. Middle names that are "last names" can be clues to research—but don't take a "clue" and make it a "fact" without something with which to back it up.

## What Does It Mean When I Say I'm 50 Years Old?

*13 February 2011*

Assume your ancestor is correct when, on 5 January 1850, he says he is 50 years old. What does that mean? He could have just turned 50 that very day, meaning he was born 5 January 1800. That would be the very youngest he could be on 5 January 1800—50 years and no days old. He could also have turned 51 the very next day, meaning he was born 6 January 1799. That would be the very oldest he could be on 5 January 1800 and still be 50, one day shy of his 51st birthday.

## True, False, and Somewhere in Between

*15 February 2011*

When analyzing any record, remember that it may be partially true and partially false. Most documents contain several statements. Rarely is a document entirely correct. One part may be true, other parts may be false. Some parts could be partially correct—the year of an event may be right, but the month may be wrong. The state may be correct, but the town may be incorrect. Keep an open mind to the very real possibility that most documents contain true statements, false statements, and statements somewhere in between. That's why it is important to transcribe each document as it is written and do the analysis elsewhere. Don't play proofreader when transcribing a document. The changes you make may not be the right ones.

## To Whom Was the Quit Claim Made?

*16 February 2011*

If you see your ancestor as a party on a quit claim deed, pay close attention to whom he was buying land from or to whom he was selling it. A high proportion of quit claim deeds are among relatives, generally to clean up an inheritance. Sometimes it can be to settle property during a divorce or to clean up property title after a dispute regarding ownership has been solved. A quit claim means you are giving up your claim, something that heirs are likely to do among themselves after the owner passes away.

## Multiple Databases for the Same Thing?

*17 February 2011*

Don't use just one database when performing searches. If there is another site that indexes the same data, their index might allow for different searches or might have included transcriptions done differently. You might not want to subscribe to one of the pay sites for the long term, but you might make a list of things you can't find on the free sites and consider subscribing to a pay-site for maybe a month. Do your searches and then let it expire or cancel it. Never rely solely on one site for all your indexes.

## Did Any Aunts Get a Widow's Pension?

*18 February 2011*

Did any of your aunts receive a Civil War pension, Revolutionary War pension, etc.? Don't think it couldn't help you in your research. If the aunt tried to qualify for a pension, she would have had to have proven her marriage. That location alone could be a clue, because if your ancestor's sister was living there, other family members could have been as well. And if the aunt couldn't find paper proof of her marriage, she might have had relatives provide affidavits testifying to the date and place of marriage. These affidavits are often made out by family members. There may be other affidavits from other family members and long-term neighbors in the application.

# If One Thing Were Not True

*20 February 2011*

Think about all that you know about your brick wall ancestor. Write them down. Now, cross one of those "facts" and pretend it is not true—even if you really think it is. How would your research approach change? What would you do differently? Where else would you look? What would happen if other "facts" were not true?

# Do You Need to Insert Some "Sicness" in Your Transcriptions?

*21 February 2011*

Remember when transcribing any document, items should be copied as they are written—wrong or not. If you see an obvious error, you may wish to insert [*sic*] after it to indicate that the mistake was not yours.

# Did They Get Off a Line?

*22 February 2011*

Is it possible that the census taker got off a line while writing up the actual census that you are using? It is possible that the enumerator got off by a line when copying the ages and didn't even notice it? If the heads of household in successive enumerations are all under the age of five, it's likely the enumerator was off a line when making his final census copy.

# Left Out Doesn't Mean Not A Child

*23 February 2011*

Just because someone is left out of an ancestor's will does not mean they were not the ancestor's child. They might have received property before the will was written or might have had a falling out with the parent. Sometimes a will may mention the child and give them a token amount of money or indicate that they were already provided for so that the child cannot say they were left out, but that doesn't always happen. The 1850 era will of Thomas Chaney in Bedford County, Pennsylvania, only mentions a handful of his ten known children and does not reference the others at all. An 1830 deed does give property and money to two of his children, but that gift is not mentioned in the will—nor are those children.

## Farmed Out at a Young Age?

*24 February 2011*

You've found your ancestors in the 1850 census, but there appear to be gaps in the ages of the children. It is possible that some died and it's possible that some are living with neighbors or other family members, perhaps helping out with children, farm work, etc. It is also possible that great-great-great-grandma didn't have any children between Henry in 1832 and Sarah in 1840. It's also possible that great-great-great-grandpa's first wife died in 1832 and he married his second wife in the late 1830s.

## Only on Paper

*26 February 2011*

More material than ever is available in digital format, either free or on a fee-based site. Remember that a significant amount of material exists only in paper form, in the original location where it was recorded. You are missing out if you only access digital images and microfilm.

## Is the Wife Listed First?

*27 February 2011*

I've seen quite a few deeds in my genealogy research. I recently located one where the wife was listed first instead of the husband. The deed references them as "Elizabeth Frame and husband." This is atypical. What it likely means is that the money to buy the house in Chicago was hers, in this case likely an inheritance from her father. It is rare to see a woman listed first in a legal record when she and her husband are both living and listed. If she is listed first, see if you can determine why.

## You Won't Always Find Everything Precisely

*28 February 2011*

There are things that researchers will not be able to pinpoint precisely. No record might exist that provides great-grandfather's exact date of birth, and March of 1874 may be as specific as you are going to get. Keep perspective about this. How crucial is having the precise day of the month or even the month of the year? Bigger concerns are that you have this ancestor tied to the right parents, sibling, spouse, children, etc. A date of birth that is not specific is not always the end of the genealogy world—unless it is key to separating two people with similar names who are about the same age. And then again, it's still about connecting them to the right people in their life.

## Is There Yet Another Marriage?

*01 March 2011*

My ancestor's second wife disappeared after his death in the 1880s. She apparently dropped off the face of the earth or was abducted by aliens. Turns out, she married after my ancestor died, thus changing her last name. If a woman disappears, remember that she could be right where she always was, just living with a new husband and a new last name.

## Homestead Proves Citizenship

*02 March 2011*

Keep in mind if your foreign-born ancestor proved a homestead claim in the United States, he had to prove citizenship. What this means is that there should be a copy of his naturalization papers in his homestead file. Where that naturalization took place could be a clue if the ancestor naturalized before he headed out to homestead.

# Were They Really Alone?

*03 March 2011*

Your female ancestor marries for the first time in her late teens or early twenties. The marriage takes place apparently several states away from where she was born. Have you looked very carefully in the area where she married for relatives of hers? Keep in mind her relatives might not be listed under her maiden name if her natural father died and her mother married again. They could be living nearby under the second husband's name. And it is always possible that what you think was the first marriage was not really the first marriage.

# Look It Up!

*04 March 2011*

If you don't know what it means, look it up. Misinterpreted terms can create even bigger brick walls for yourself and other researchers. Make certain you know key dates in local history for the locations where you are researching. When were counties formed, when were streets renumbered, when did the courthouse burn, etc.? Don't guess. Once in a while, our lack of knowledge can aggravate the problem.

# Google Maps is Not Perfect

*07 March 2011*

Google maps does not always get every location correct. Some cities had renumbering or renaming of streets and there is always the possibility that a house number from 1880 is not the same as the house number today.

# Track When You Searched That Online Source

*08 March 2011*

Online databases change—sometimes they add data or make corrections. Part of tracking your search should include the date an online database was accessed. Then you can compare the date of an update with the date of your search and know whether you need to search the database again or not. That's assuming the website is clear in when updates are made or what those updates contain. Many do not make users aware of changes.

## Were They Dead Then?

*09 March 2011*

Recently I spent a fair amount of time trying to find someone in the 1860 census. Various spellings and other search techniques were of no help. I was reasonably certain of the location where the person was living and a manual search of that area brought no results. A review of the probate of the individual's actual will indicated it was admitted to probate in 1855 instead of the 1865 that I had transcribed and entered in my database. Problem solved.

## Search for Name Abbreviations

*10 March 2011*

It was late and I was trying to search for a person I knew I had already found in an 1860 census but had forgotten to save or create a citation for—William Brice. After several attempts, there he was, listed as Wm. Brice. Don't forget that some individuals may be enumerated under abbreviated names. Wildcard searches do not always catch these alternate names. Will* certainly would not catch Wm.

## Could that "l" be a "t?"

*11 March 2011*

Think about that letter you think is an "l" (lower case "L"). Could it actually be a "t" that simply didn't get crossed? Even if the creator of the record crossed every other "t," he could have left one uncrossed. And Soundex searches won't catch it when a "t" and an "l" have been switched. Wildcard searches will if you have the wildcard operator in the correct place.

## Multiple Handwriting on One Document

*12 March 2011*

Look carefully at that next original document you see. Does it appear that the handwriting was all done at the same time by the same person? Or were things written over time? My grandfather's 1903 birth certificate was apparently filled out at three different times based upon the handwriting and slight differences in the color of the ink. One person apparently wrote the bulk of the document when it was recorded in November of 1903. Someone else wrote Grandpa's last name in later—the handwriting is significantly different. Someone else wrote in his first and middle name—the ink color is slightly different, as is the handwriting. Sometimes these things are not apparent on a black and white copy or a transcription.

## Search for Locations-Not Just Names

*13 March 2011*

Are you searching a digital version of that county history, biography book, etc.? Try searching for locations as well as names. It can be a great way to see what other biographies and similar material in the book mentions locations where your ancestor was from. A search of an Illinois county history for "coshocton ohio" located several references to people from that county besides my ancestor. A great way to get names of potential former neighbors, associates, and possible relatives.

## Consider Something You Don't Need

*15 March 2011*

Sometimes it might be worth it to order a record you think you don't need. My grandmother's brother died in the 1930s with little estate to settle up (except for a car and a small amount of cash). On a whim, I ordered a copy of his estate record. There was a paper in the file signed by all his siblings and his mother, waiving their inheritance. It didn't provide me any new information, but it was neat to have the signature of my grandmother, her five siblings, and her mother all on one document. And if I had not already known he was divorced, the fact that he had no surviving spouse would have been a big clue, too!

## Look Before and After

*16 March 2011*

When you locate a deed for an ancestor or relative, look a few pages before and after to see if other documents were recorded by the relative at the same time. Going to the courthouse might have been more than a day trip and your relative might have grouped his courthouse work to save time.

## Search Ledgers and Not Just Packets

*18 March 2011*

In courthouses that have them, genealogists often focus on the packet of papers—court papers, probate papers, etc. Don't forget that some information may be recorded in court ledgers, registers, etc. The packet of loose papers is great, but don't forget that some details may only be in the record books.

## Changed Denomination Late in Life?

*19 March 2011*

Does your ancestor evaporate from church records late in their life? Don't assume it is because they died—perhaps they changed denominations. Grandpa might not always have been a Methodist and Grandma might not have always been a Catholic. Change does happen. When they retired, a set of ancestors changed churches and switched from Lutheran to Presbyterian. The reason? The town they retired to had two churches: Roman Catholic and Presbyterian.

## Power of the Widow?

*20 March 2011*

This phrase generally means that a widow had more control over real property if she stayed single than if she married after her husband's death. During the time when women had fewer legal rights, a widow would have the right to a widow's dower in a portion of his real property (non-transferable and good for her life time only) or a husband might give his wife a life estate in all his property after his death and then bequeath it to his children (who were often hers as well) after her death. In some cases the husband may have chosen to have the life estate end if the widow remarried after her husband's death. Others may not have imposed that restriction on their surviving wife.

The life estate meant the widow could not sell, mortgage, or bequeath the property. It also meant that if she married again, a subsequent husband could not gain control of the property. This served to protect the widow from a subsequent husband who might marry her to gain control of her real estate. The widow had "power" over the management of the property for as long as she lived.

## Copy All Those Column Headings

*22 March 2011*

When making a copy of any record, make certain you take note of all column headings if the record appears in a ledger or record book that uses them. It's imperative if the record is in a foreign language, but still important with records in any language. One does not want to interpret information incorrectly, and that can easily happen if column headings are not recorded or transcribed when the record is originally viewed. Relying on memory does not work. Copying these items when you have access to the record saves the time of having to go back and get them later.

# There Are No Secondary Sources in Genealogy

*23 March 2011*

In current genealogy practice, the adjectives "primary" and "secondary" refer to information not to sources (sources are original or derivative). Primary information is given by someone who had reasonable firsthand knowledge of something. Information provided by others whose knowledge was not primary is said to be secondary. Any source can have primary and secondary information, depending upon who provided it and how they came to know it. If I am with my grandmother when she dies, I may be the informant on her death certificate. The information I provide on her date and place of death would be primary information—I have firsthand knowledge as I was there. The information I provide on her parents would be secondary as I do not have firsthand knowledge of her birth—I wasn't there.

# Did They Appear When Someone Died?

*24 March 2011*

If there is a relative who "disappeared" after a certain point in time, determine if there were any estates they might have inherited from after that time. Was there a parent who died after the "disappearance?" Would the disappearing person have inherited part of an estate after they went "poof?" If so, the settlement of that estate would have required that they be found or at least their absence be explained. A cousin died in Illinois 1940s with no children, and court records go into detail about the searches made in California and Colorado for his brother who went "poof" in the 1920s. The judge ended up declaring him dead so that his children could inherit from their uncle and his estate could be closed.

# Books on Collateral Families

*26 March 2011*

Is there a book on a collateral branch of your family that may provide information on your direct lineage? A book on the in-laws of one of my aunts contained significant information on her own family of origin even though they were not the focus of the book. It pays to look.

## Why Was That Record Created?

*28 March 2011*

The vast majority of records genealogists use were not created for genealogists. Probate records were created to settle estates, land records were used to document land transfers, census record were used to collect statistical information about citizens (and in the US to apportion representatives,) church records were kept to document that certain sacraments had been performed, etc. If you don't know why a record was created, find out. Learning why may help you understand and interpret the item you have found.

## Tools of the Trade

*29 March 2011*

Are there occupational clues hidden in the inventory of your ancestor's estate? Sometimes it can be difficult determining the occupation of your pre-1850 ancestor. The inventory of the personal items in his estate may hold a clue. Be careful about drawing conclusions and compare to other inventories to see what makes your ancestor's different—everyone had kitchen utensils and a chamber pot.

Occupational clues may be contained in other records as well. Many European church records provide the occupation of the father to help distinguish between men of the same name (and to indicate social status in some cases). Land deeds in some locations may mention the occupation of the buyer and seller.

# Reading It Cold

*30 March 2011*

Remember that in many cases, the indexer indexing the record you are using was not familiar with the names in the area where the records were created. In most cases, they are reading the names "cold." Keep that in mind when formulating searches and contemplating alternate spellings. You may know what it says. Someone else may not.

# Clues in the First Names of Neighbors

*01 April 2011*

Always look at the neighbors. Sometimes the clues are pretty obvious. In 1900, my relative Henry Jacobs Fecht is enumerated as a father-in-law in his son-in-law's household. The adjacent house has an eighteen-year-old male named Henry Jacobs Fecht. Seems highly coincidental and worth looking into. Look at the first names of members of adjacent households, not just the last names. Are there clues in those names? Are there any slightly unusual first names that are repeated in nearby households? If two nearby households both have a son named Ebenezer and a daughter named Temperance, there may be a connection between the families even if they don't have the same last name. In this Fecht example, it turns out the older Henry Jacobs Fecht is the grandfather of the younger one.

# Take A Moment to Stop Gathering

*02 April 2011*

For those times when locating information seems easy, stop and take time to analyze what you have already located. Get off the websites, get off the internet, stop checking your email, stop gathering more information, etc. and look at what you have. Sketch out relationships, make chronologies, and make timelines. You may see errors you didn't see before or opportunities you have overlooked. Either way, you're better off. Sometimes it pays to stop collecting for a while and do some analyzing.

## Making A Mark Doesn't Mean They Were Illiterate
*02 April 2011*

Remember that just because your ancestor signs their "mark" on a document doesn't mean they were illiterate. In some cases, a person might have been told to "make their mark" which was unique to them and, as long as it was witnessed, legally binding. And because they were

told to "make their mark," that is what they did. If your ancestor was ill and on their death bed when they signed their will, making their mark might have been all they could do. I have several ancestors who signed numerous documents throughout their lifetime, but made their "mark" on their will, generally because they were advanced in years. Be wary of making conclusions about your ancestor's literacy based on the presence or absence of one signature on one document. Some people could "draw their name," even if they really could not read.

## Sections, Quartersections, and Congressional Townships
*03 April 2011*

In most areas of the United States where land was surveyed under the Rectangular Survey System of land measurement, a section is 640 acres, a quartersection is 160 acres, and a Congressional township is 6 miles on a side. These are theoretical sizes and measurements and can easily vary slightly given local terrain. Congressional Townships are not the same as civil townships, although in some cases their boundaries may be the same. Civil townships serve governmental functions. Congressional townships are generally used in land description. If you are doing research in a state that uses sections and townships, and your ancestors were property owners, these are terms with which you should be familiar as legal descriptions of property will frequently use these terms.

## Why Did They Wait?

*04 April 2011*

The widow dies and three daughters jointly inherit twelve acres in Ohio during the 1850s. One daughter apparently pre-deceased her mother and left children of her own. The two surviving daughters sign deeds over to their brother at about the same time as each other, probably shortly after the mother's death. The deceased daughter's heirs wait several years to sign their deed. Why? I'm not certain, but my guess is that they waited for all the deceased daughter's children to come of age so that they could legally sign the deed. Minors can't execute deeds. To transfer the land before all the children reached the age of majority, a guardian would have been necessary. That would have meant court action and additional expenses. It may have been easier and cheaper to just wait until the youngest child of the pre-deceased daughter reached the legal age to execute a deed in their own name.

## Recorded in the Margin

*05 April 2011*

Always look in the margins of courthouse record books, census pages, or any record you find. Look on the front and back of every document. Look over the entire packet that contains loose papers. In general, look everywhere. If you find comments in the margin of the document, they were probably written there for a reason. In the case of mortgages, you may find an acknowledgement on the record copy of the mortgage that the mortgage was released—signed by the holder of the note. Other records can easily contain annotations that can sometimes be relevant.

## Coparceners

*06 April 2011*

The word "coparcener," generally speaking, means joint heirs. Siblings, whose father dies without a will, may be referred to as "coparceners" of his real estate, meaning that they own it jointly. They each have a share of the whole, not a specific part of the real estate. To have their part clearly marked typically requires court action (often called a partition suit) or at least complete agreement among the heirs.

## Stuck People Should Read

*07 April 2011*

If you get stuck on an ancestor, read a county or local history of the area. It probably won't mention your ancestor, but reading and learning something about the history of the place your ancestor lived will at least make you more knowledgeable about the location. It just may spark a research idea. And if you've read the county history—read a local newspaper for a week if it's a daily and for a month if it's a weekly. That's more background that won't hurt your research.

## Is There a Form They Actually Filled Out Themselves?

*08 April 2011*

Some records we use were not filled out by our ancestors—someone else, perhaps with less knowledge, answered the questions. At times it can be difficult to get a record where the information was directly provided by the person and not through an intermediary. My big break on my wife's grandmother came not from her death certificate, which was filled out by her children, but instead her SS-5 form (application for a Social Security Number). The grandmother filled out that form herself in the 1960s and gave a different name for her father than what her children had put on her death certificate thirty years later. It is very likely that she never thought anyone would ever see the record. If possible, find something for which the person actually provided the information. It may contain different details than what other members of the family had to say about them.

## Clerk's Copy

*12 April 2011*

Sometimes called the record copy, this is the official recorded copy of a document, usually made in the local records office. This copy is usually considered the legal equivalent of the original copy.

## One Office, Many Courts

*13 April 2011*

In some counties, the court records office may hold records of several different courts. Make certain you have accessed the records of each court you need. There may be an equity court, a criminal court, a probate court, and other courts depending upon the location and the time period. Each court will have their own set of records and indexes. Find out what court had jurisdiction over the type of case for which you are looking—don't assume you know, particularly if it is an area with which you are not familiar.

Always make certain you are accessing all the court records and the records of every court. One way I do this is to look in the index for names that begin with the letter "S." There are always many names. There should be a column in the index for "type of action." If you go through the letter "S" and see foreclosures, liens, etc. but *no divorces, no bastardry cases, no partition suits,* then there is probably another court with a separate set of records that hears this type of cases. It would be odd if no one with the last name of Smith ever got divorced—not to mention all the other last names that begin with "S."

## Wife Disappearing from the Releases?

*14 April 2011*

When a husband sells property and is married, there should be an acknowledgment by the wife that she knows about the sale and releases her dower interest in the property. Pay attention to these acknowledgments. The absence of one usually indicates the wife is deceased—a potential clue. And a "new name" appearing on the dower release likely means that the previous wife has died and the husband has remarried. Keep nicknames and diminutives in mind when drawing these conclusions, however. An 1800 deed may reference a wife named Sarah and that same woman may be referred to as Sally in 1820. The wife was supposed to be examined in private to make certain she really agreed to the sale of the property. Of course if she said "no," her husband was going to find out pretty quickly so the privacy was not so private.

## Children's Guardian?

*15 April 2011*

If your male ancestor died with even a small amount of real estate or enough personal property, there might be a guardianship case for his children. The mother likely was the guardian of the child's person, but someone else might have been appointed guardian of the child's estate. Pay close attention to the name of this person. It might have been a male relative or, in some cases, a stepfather, and that relationship may never be spelled out in the documents.

# Chapter 16: All I Need Is Love, Crossing a Line, and Joseph Conversions

## Did Your Ancestor Record His Notch?

*16 April 2011*

In frontier areas, when livestock roamed without fences, farmers often had their own peculiar notch they used to identify their hogs or cattle. Records of these notches may be found at the local courthouse, recorded with other public records. In areas where branding livestock was a common practice, one may find records of brands. At the very least the image makes for a nice illustration.

## Are You Violating the Laws of Biology or Physics?

*18 April 2011*

Look at information you have compiled or located. Look at it closely. If to make the story fit, you have to violate laws of biology (dead people do not typically reproduce, people who have not yet been born do not have children, etc.) or the laws of physics (travelling 400 miles on land within two days in 1820, etc.), then there is a problem. Violating common sense is not usually advised either.

## Do You Only Have an Abstract?

*19 April 2011*

Is there a brick wall problem where you have an abstract of a record instead of the complete record? Is it possible the abstract includes a word of phrase transcribed incorrectly, or a key phrase that has been omitted? It's possible that a detail the abstracter considered trivial (and left out as a result) is key to your problem. Make certain you've got the complete records on all records for your "brick wall." A small omission can sometimes make a great deal of difference.

## They Really Did Not Care How It Was Spelled

*22 April 2011*

In modern society, for a variety of reasons, we are concerned about how our name gets spelled. Our ancestors were not so concerned. They didn't worry about the various agencies, companies, and levels of government that had records on them that needed to be consistent. I'm typing an 1820 era Kentucky court case and the last name of Bonham is spelled Berham, Benham, Burham, etc. One document often spells the name several different ways on the same sheet of paper. The key is that the name should sound the same and refer to the same person. Transcribe the name how it is spelled. Do not standardize the spelling. One reason is that the variant spellings give insight into how the name was pronounced or heard. Another reason is that if someone sees you "correcting the spelling" when you transcribe a document, they might wonder what else you fixed along the way.

It's fine to standardize a name spelling when writing about your ancestor or in compiling the family genealogy. That is less confusing for the reader. When the variants are significantly different from the name, it's also helpful to your reader if you explain why you think they refer to the same person.

## All the Consideration I Need Is Your Love

*24 April 2011*

If a deed of transfer for a piece of property or other item indicates that the only consideration is "love and affection," there is a likely relationship between the seller and buyer on the property. It might not even be technically correct to refer to the grantee as a buyer in this case (recipient may be a better word). The relationship between the parties might not be stated. Similarly, if the amount of the consideration on a deed is a token amount (a dollar, five dollars, etc.) that also might be a clue as to a potential relationship between the individuals involved. Deeds that say a "dollar and other valuable consideration" are potentially different. That "other valuable consideration" may be referring to a mortgage or other document also recorded on the property. In that case, the token amount of a dollar serves a different purpose and there may not necessarily be a relationship among the parties involved.

## Witness Not a Beneficiary

*25 April 2011*

Witnesses on a document do not have to be related to the person signing the document. It is a genealogy myth that they must be related. For wills, witnesses usually cannot be heirs or beneficiaries of the will. A witness just has to be of the age of majority and know the person signing the document. That's it.

One potential exception to this is when the individual signing the document cannot read the document. The witnesses may have been individuals the signer trusted to read it to make certain it said what the signer actually thought it said.

## Look for that Cemetery in a Directory

*26 April 2011*

Having trouble finding that 100-year old cemetery? If it is in a location that published city directories, see if the directory had a list of cemeteries. Might be that a directory has an "old name" for a cemetery that's not in modern materials, reference a location that's not showing up in current directories, etc.

## Did They Have Relatives Already Here?

*27 April 2011*

A relative insisted that our common ancestor had no "family" in the area where he settled in the 1840s and stated that he was the only one in his family to migrate to the Midwest. For years I took her at her word, largely because I had not adequately researched his family of origin beyond his siblings.

The no other family members was not correct. What the teller of the story might have meant was that no one in James' immediate family of siblings settled near him. That was true. Always look for relatives in the new area where your ancestor settled, despite what the relatives today may insist is true. It's also possible that their definition of a word or two may differ from yours.

## Look at the Act

*29 April 2011*

When viewing anyone's military pension, look at the act under which he or she was applying. Look at what types of service qualified under the act, the length of required service, etc. If a widow is applying, see if the act mentions length of time married, whether she could have married him after the war, or other variables. There may be clues about your ancestor hiding in the act under which the application was made.

## What Have You Overlooked?

*30 April 2011*

I didn't bother to get the will of the ancestor for one of my wife's families. In fact, I never looked for it. The records weren't microfilmed and I already knew "everything" about the family from other records. If there was a will, it wasn't going to tell me anything I didn't already know. Wrong! The will was short— "everything to my wife." The order probating the will mentioned all the heirs, including a child in a mental institution, complete with the institution's name and address. If possible, don't leave records ignored because you "know everything." There may still be clues in those materials, because you still don't know everything.

## The Rules Change When You Cross A Line

*01 May 2011*

When you cross any political line, including county, state, province, territory, and nation, the laws and recordkeeping system may change. In some cases, the change can be significant. Even when crossing states/provincial lines, the laws regarding what is recorded and how it is recorded may change. Learn about the new area's records before you assume that Virginia in 1760 is just like Nebraska in 1860. That's something of an extreme example, but it hopefully makes the point.

## Get to Those Stones Now!

*03 May 2011*

Are there any pre-1900 tombstones you have not transcribed or photographed? Look through your records, your database, etc. Put getting the information from the stone on your priority list. Old stones do not last forever and the information may literally fade away before you get to it. Be careful relying totally on published transcriptions. Sometimes in an attempt to be helpful, people added information to the "transcription" that really was not on the stone. Do you have any stones you have neglected?

## Estate Receipts May Have Signatures and More

*03 May 2011*

Looking for an ancestor's signature? Is there an estate they would have been an heir to? Perhaps there is a signed receipt in the packet of estate papers. Actual receipts won't usually appear in the order books and journals (although their names and amounts may be listed in an accounting), but some locations have the actual packets of papers. That's one place to get a signature. There may also be a notation as to where the individual was living at the time they received the money as well.

## Don't Neglect the Online Trees

*04 May 2011*

A variety of websites have submitted family trees. Virtually all of them contain errors. Some of them contain many errors. But don't ignore them completely. Sometimes even a very careless researcher stumbles upon something that we have overlooked. Don't take anything in the online trees as gospel without documenting it elsewhere, but keep in mind the possibility that one of them may have the clue that you need. It is also possible that some of them may raise your blood pressure when you see the errors.

## How That Information Got on The Stone

*05 May 2011*

I'm not talking about a chisel. Think about how great-grandpa's information got on his tombstone. Someone thought they knew when he was born and so they told the stonecutter. Probably that same person provided the death information. Maybe. If the stone was put up years after great-grandpa died, it is possible the stone has the wrong date of death. The date of birth could be wrong as well. Tombstones are usually original sources providing primary information for the date of death, unless you can clearly tell the stone was erected years after the person died. The main thing is to transcribe it exactly as it is written. Your discussion of why you think it is wrong (or right) should be done in your notes. Just because it is inscribed in stone does not mean it had to be correct. It's on stone because someone paid to have the stone inscribed.

## Land Warrant versus Land Patents

*07 May 2011*

A Federal land warrant usually entitles someone to a certain acreage of property in the Federal domain, without giving any real specifics about where that property is located or transferring actual title. These warrants are issued for several reasons, with the most common being a reward for previous military service. A land patent transfers title to a specific piece of property to an individual. Those are broad generalizations and before interpreting anything in a land warrant or land patent, learn more about them in the area and time period where they were issued. Some of the original colonies issued them, some early US states issued them, and the US government issued them. Only those in the latter category are Federal records. What's true about one may not necessarily be one-hundred percent true about another.

## Be Patient with Newer Genealogists

*08 May 2011*

Remember that everyone was a beginning genealogist at one point or another. Give that newer genealogist some time to "learn the ropes." An extra dose of patience may be necessary if you are both researching a family where people married more than once, had spouses with similar names, etc. Those situations can tax an experienced genealogist and are more difficult for someone new to research.

## Avoid That 21st Century Mind

*09 May 2011*

It may be difficult to do, but remember when reading or analyzing any document that unless it was created during your adult lifetime, there might be some cultural, historical, economic, or legal events impacting that document *of which you are unaware.* Don't interpret a 19th century document with a 21st century mind.

And remember that even if the document was created during your lifetime, there still may be some things about it you don't know.

## What It Says—Not What It "Should" Say

*10 May 2011*

Remember that transcribers of records are supposed to copy a record or a source the way it is written—not what they think the record should say. If grandma's name is Susannah and her marriage record lists her as Susan, transcribe it as Susan. If grandma gave the wrong place of birth on her marriage record don't "fix it" when you make the transcription, copy it as it is on the record. You can (and should) make a notation somewhere that the information is incorrect, and state how you know it is wrong, but don't edit and correct what was on an original record.

Also keep in mind that most archival agencies jobs are to preserve the records that they have—*not to correct them.* They are not going to process your request to have a date of birth changed on a 1932 death certificate.

## Google that Old Occupation

*14 May 2011*

Can't find anything on an occupation? Consider typing it into *GoogleBooks* at books.google.com. You may discover more than you realized. Also consider typing it into *Google Images* images.google.com. Don't neglect searching for that occupation in old newspapers that have full-text search capabilities as well.

## Are You Stereotyping Your Ancestors?

*17 May 2011*

Are you assuming your ancestor acted like the typical Irishman, the typical German, etc.? Doing so may cause you to believe things about your ancestors that were not true and make brick walls for yourself. There are a variety of reasons why your ancestor may not follow typical ethnic customs—don't assume ancestral behaviors for which you have no evidence. Most of us don't like it when others stereotype us—let's not stereotype our ancestors either.

## Marriage Bann

*18 May 2011*

A marriage bann is an ecclesiastical or civil announcement of an upcoming marriage. Ecclesiastical marriage banns are typically made in church the three Sundays before the wedding. Civil announcements may be done in a variety of places with a similar time frame. Both were to let people be aware of the marriage so if there was a reason it should not take place (*eg.* the groom was already married) that reason could be made public. Publication of the banns does not mean the marriage took place. Sometimes the banns have the effect of banning the marriage. That was the reason for having them in the first place.

## Cite the Cemetery Site

*19 May 2011*

"Site" is a location. "Cite" means to indicate where a piece of information was obtained. You should cite the cemetery site when referencing a tombstone. The tombstone site is where the tombstone was located and your citation for the tombstone site should be specific enough that someone else could get to the site using your citation (GPS coordinates, address, township and section number [if rural], location within the cemetery, etc.).

## Two Books in One Volume

*20 May 2011*

To save money, libraries may bind more than one softcover book in a hardcover binding, particularly when the softcover books are part of a series. Make certain you aren't just looking in the index of the "last book" in the bound book. It can be easy to overlook the index of the "first" book when two are bound together.

## Did Someone Convert a Joseph?

*21 May 2011*

I was using a transcription of vital records that indicated a relative was named Jas. I assumed the reference was to James and was searching for that name. Turns out the record that was transcribed had used "Jos." for Joseph and the transcriber made the "o" an "a." Copy down what the transcriber wrote, but keep in mind that they might have incorrectly copied the record—or that the record was difficult to read and that the transcriber did the best they could. Also remember that certain homemade abbreviations could have stood for more than one name. In this case I know the name is actually Joseph. It could have been Josiah.

## Do You Know What You Are Looking At?

*22 May 2011*

A relative was great about sending me stuff while she was actively researching and I really appreciated it. She always indicated the volume number of the courthouse book and the page number of the information. The problem is that she sometimes made up book titles that made sense to her and occasionally they aren't accurate. She extracted accurately but sometimes left out key details. If you are using Family History microfilm of original records, look at the "title sheet" that starts each record and use that for your title if you don't know what the book is. If it's an original ledger, see what is on the cover or the spine. You never know, you might want to go back some day and review it yourself.

## Did You Copy Selected Materials the First Time?

*23 May 2011*

Some of my research was done back in the day when making a paper copy of every record was cost prohibitive. Some of those records have now been digitized by the Family History Library. I've been going back and, in some cases, making a digital copy of the entire record, getting lots of really interesting information. Is there something you only partially copied years ago that perhaps now you could copy more extensively?

## He Was Formerly Late or Was He Late Formerly?

*24 May 2011*

Remember that "late" does not necessarily mean dead. "Late of Harford County" can simply mean that the person used to live there. In some legal and other documents, "late" means formerly. Deceased usually means dead, however!

## Grandchildren's Biographies?

*25 May 2011*

If the time period and locations are appropriate, have you looked for biographies of all the grandchildren of your "problem" ancestor? It is always possible one of them mentioned a detail about their grandfather in their own biography—and that could be a big clue. Searching for the grandfather by using his name might not work if he is only referred to as "grandfather" in the biography and never named specifically. There could be information on him in the publication even though his name does not actually appear in it.

## Are Their 1850 Neighbors the Same as the 1750 Neighbors?

*26 May 2011*

I have a family that moved from Virginia into Kentucky in the 1790-1800 time frame. The interesting thing is that the names of neighboring families to my ancestors in 1750 Virginia are the same names I see as their Kentucky neighbors in 1850. I've got another set of German families that essentially "transplanted" a village from northern Germany to Illinois in the mid to late 1800s. Some people tend to stick together even when they move. Sometimes they all end up related.

## Widow's Probate? Or Not.

*27 May 2011*

In locations and time periods where women had few property and legal rights, there are not often estate settlements if the wife dies first. However, if the wife dies last, always look for an estate settlement, a quit claim deed, non-probate court action, or some type of settlement to tidy up the estate. People assume that because women who die first don't often have estate or probate records that they won't when they die last, either. That's not necessarily true.

## Ledgers Versus Certificates

*28 May 2011*

Keep in mind some counties may have ledgers with birth information and separate birth certificates. I looked in the birth certificates for two of my grandparents and did not find them, but when I looked in the birth register—there they were. It pays to make certain you have searched everything.

# Chapter 17: Leaving Family, Dead Proofing, One Little Entry

## Who Is Alive?

*29 May 2011*

Think about who is listed on a document and who that document implies is alive at the time the document is written. A will mentioning children usually means that the children are alive at the time the will is written. There's no guarantee the children are still alive when the will is admitted to probate.

## Avoiding Abbreviations

*31 May 2011*

Use abbreviations sparingly. Does "w/o James Rampley" mean "wife of James Rampley" or "without James Rampley?" If the reference appears on a tombstone, the meaning is likely obvious. But remember, what is one person's "obvious" is someone else's "huh?" Abbreviations can easily confuse—use them with care and avoid them if at all possible.

## Did It Leave the Family?

*01 June 2011*

My aunt was the third wife of her fifth husband. In her Civil War pension application, she mentions having his family bible which included death dates of his wife and others. I'm wondering what happened to the Bible upon her death. It's very possible it actually went to her family and left her husband's family altogether. Could this have happened to one of your family items? It might be worth contacting descendants of an ancestor's stepchild to see if they have any knowledge of materials of this type.

## Notary Statements on Deeds

*02 June 2011*

If a family sold a deceased parent's land after the parent died, not all of the children might have lived near where the property was located. They might have been sent copies of deed, told to acknowledge it in front of a local official, and mail back signed documents. That acknowledgement would have been recorded with the actual deed in the records office where the property was located. That's how a deed for my ancestor's White County, Indiana, farm in the 1860s told me the counties in Iowa, Illinois, and Louisiana where his children were living at the time of the deed. The acknowledgements were done in front of a local official where they lived and that local official indicated the county or location in which he held office. Don't neglect to read the acknowledgements on a deed—they may hold clues as to where heirs are living.

## Execution Date, Acknowledgement Date, and Recording Date

*03 June 2011*

A deed may have the date it was signed, the date it was acknowledged, and the date it was recorded. Make certain you indicate which is which. They can be clues in some cases. A husband and wife executed a deed in 1814 in Kentucky and by the time it was acknowledged a month later, the wife is listed as a widow. This allowed me to approximate the date of death for the husband.

## Coloring the Truth

*04 June 2011*

Remember when reading those widow's pensions, that it was in the widow's interest to make herself, "poor, destitute, and without support." Statements should always be interpreted with the thought that the claimant might have "shaded" comments to make things go in their favor. This is not to say that some widows were not destitute and in need of support, but some of them may have tried to create an impression that was not consistent with reality. Same thing applies to statements made in divorce records.

## 1890 Veterans and Widows Schedule

*05 June 2011*

Don't forget that there was a special 1890 US census enumeration that included Civil War veterans and Civil War veteran's widows. Returns for states whose name begins with the letters A-K were mostly destroyed. These have been microfilmed by the National Archives, and NARA microfilm M123 and are online at *FamilySearch*.

## Which Part Is Correct?

*06 June 2011*

Even if an entry in a death certificate or other record appears to be incorrect, keep in mind that, on the surface, it can be hard to determine what's right and what's not. A relative's death certificate listed her mother's maiden name as "Mrs. Little." Confusing—and I originally thought that maybe the "mother" had married after the father's death and that "Mrs. Little" was her name at death instead of her maiden name. Turns out Liddell was her maiden name. And the "Mrs." reference? Who knows? It easily could have been an error or a miswritten "Miss."

## Delayed Certificates

*07 June 2011*

Always look for copies of delayed certificates, particularly for births. Sometimes if a birth certificate was not filed when the event took place, one will be filed later. This is most common when the person needed their birth certificate and realized they did not have one. There may be copies of affidavits, statements, or references to other records as a part of the delayed record and these records may be filed separately from the originals. These are usually filed where the birth took place, but there are always exceptions.

## Ask a Local

*08 June 2011*

You can obtain a lot of information via libraries, microfilm, published books, etc. You can get help from people who have never stepped foot near where your ancestor actually lived. And sometimes it is extremely helpful to ask a local who grew up in the area and has first-hand, on-site experience there. They may know about unpublished local sources that are difficult to access or have other tricks up their sleeve based upon years of experience with local families and records. They are also more likely to know local records officials as well.

## Individual Volumes Indexed

*09 June 2011*

I was using an index to land records that covered the first fifty or so years of the county's land records. One index entry was difficult to read. The volume number was legible, but the page number wasn't. Afraid I'd have to go page by page through the entire volume, I viewed the volume and there in the front of it was an index to just that volume, giving me the actual page number. The clerk compiled indexes to each volume as they were recorded and, years later, a more comprehensive index was created.

## The Dead Don't Proof Their Obituaries

*10 June 2011*

Think about who might have written the obituary of Grandma that appeared in the newspaper. Was it a family member with "issues?" Was it someone who wanted certain people left out? Was it someone concerned with being entirely accurate? Unless you were involved firsthand in the planning of the funeral and the writing of the obituary, you might not really know who wrote the obit. And who wrote it makes all the difference.

## Age of Majority

*11 June 2011*

If your ancestor had a guardian appointed, look at when the guardian was released. It should be a clue as to approximately when the person for whom the guardian was appointed had reached the age of majority—typically eighteen for females and twenty-one for males. A clue as to approximate year of birth.

## From a Lawyer to a Sawyer in Two Seconds

*12 June 2011*

Is that "S" an "L" or is that "L" an "S?" These two uppercase letters are easy to confuse. That's why when looking for Sargents I always remember to look for Largents as well. There are other letters that can be confused as well. Could your Feather family be hiding with some Leathers?

## Did History Move Your Ancestor?

*13 June 2011*

Never assume that your relative was too insignificant to have been affected by historical events. A step-ancestor who was a native of Canada decided that the American Civil War was the prime time to leave the state of Missouri and return to his native country. He just went "poof," and the Civil War was the probable reason why.

## Just the Mother

*14 June 2011*

Remember that the only parent who has to be present at the birth of a child is the mother. The dad had to be around nine months earlier but could easily have been dead or moved on by the time the child was born.

## Double Check—It May Make a Difference

*15 June 2011*

I assumed that a genealogist I had known for ages and who was usually right had correctly transcribed a date from a Virginia land record. When I reviewed the record myself, the date had been transcribed 10 years incorrectly. It was an easy mistake. In this case, the year made a difference as it was used in part of an estimate of someone's year of death. We can all easily make mistakes. It pays to check your own work as well as someone else's. Sometimes mistakes are minor and sometimes they are not.

## Did They Move Constantly?

*16 June 2011*

Don't assume your ancestor moved infrequently. Some people did move rarely and others moved every few years. It might have just been your ancestor's wanderlust that kept him or her moving constantly. It could have been the local law. A relative of mine moved at least a dozen times between 1850 and 1890, living in three different states and numerous counties. The moves are meticulously detailed in her Civil War widow's pension application. And she very well could have moved a few more that simply were not documented in the file.

## Don't Just Show Up

*17 June 2011*

If you are travelling a distance to do research, do more than just make certain the records office will be open when you are planning to arrive. Find out if there are any days to "avoid" using the facility. Determine what the policies are for the use of digital cameras and cellphones. If you arrive when offices are being remodeled, accessing things may be difficult. You may be told to wait to come until "Gertrude comes back from vacation. She knows where everything is." It's not always possible to schedule a visit perfectly, but sometimes you can maximize the chances you have the best research experience possible.

## Read Something Unrelated to Your Research

*21 June 2011*

Every so often, read an article, blog post, etc. about a family or location completely unrelated to your personal research. You likely won't find information on your own family, but sometimes reading about something with which you are unfamiliar gets you thinking "outside the box "on your own family and causes inspiration to strike. And sometimes it just gets you out of that rut.

## How Are They Filed?

*23 June 2011*

Not every location organizes records in the same way. A marriage index indicated my wife's great-grandparents were married in Burlington, Iowa. I had the date, the location, and their names. I figured with the date it would not be difficult to find their actual marriage record. When viewing the records on microfilm, I assumed they were filmed in order of license number, or perhaps by date. I looked and they seemed to be in random order. Then I realized that the records had been sorted by the name of the groom!

## What Did It Require?

*24 June 2011*

You've found your ancestor in a personal property tax list? What was required to be in the tax list? Did the person have to be a certain age, have a certain amount of personal property, etc.? If you don't know the criteria for appearing on the list, you may be interpreting something incorrectly.

## You Better Browse

*25 June 2011*

Search boxes that allow us to quickly find census and other records have changed the way genealogists locate many records. However, there is still an advantage to browsing through that census record when one family has been located using an index. Read other names on the same page and adjacent pages. There may be other family members you did not think to look for, or whose names are so mangled they were not located using indexes. Also pay attention to the places of birth for these near neighbors—they may have followed the same path of migration as your ancestor as well.

## Did You Skip the Introduction?

*26 June 2011*

Skipping the introduction to a book, microfilm, or any record can create research problems and make brick walls even worse. Declarations of intent were damaged badly in a 19th century fire in Hamilton County, Ohio. The intentions were copied from the damaged originals into a new series of record books and those copied records were kept and eventually microfilmed. A cover sheet on the microfilm indicated potential difficulties with the records. If I had just skipped to the entry I needed, I never would have learned that it was believed that a significant number (never specifically stated) had errors. And that was something I need to know. Don't just jump to the index or the page you need. Authors don't just create introductions and prefaces to fill space.

## Leave an Audit Trail

*27 June 2011*

I know not everyone uses a research log, but at least try to leave yourself an audit trail or enough breadcrumbs to retrack your research steps. It can be exciting to be finding new information, but to go back later and remember why something was obtained or how this new person fit into the overall family scheme can be difficult. Do something (type up notes, send yourself emails) to record why you were doing what you were doing as you were doing it. Sometimes the reasons are obvious, but other times they are not.

## Not Just That One Little Entry

*29 June 2011*

When copying or scanning an entry from a record, particularly one that is handwritten free form in some type of journal, copy at least the entire page on which the entry appears. Copy a page before and after if possible. It makes it easier later to interpret handwriting and the entry itself, particularly if the person who wrote the record abbreviated, had difficult to read handwriting, etc.

## They Won't Give It If You Don't Ask

*30 June 2011*

Years ago, I wrote a county in Virginia and asked for the marriage register entry for my ancestors. The county office sent me a copy of their 1798 entry in the marriage register. I didn't ask for anything else and they didn't send anything else. Imagine my surprise when a relative sent me copies of the corresponding marriage bonds. I asked her where she got them and the reply was the same courthouse where the marriage register copy had been obtained. The difference was that she knew to also ask for the marriage bonds and at that time, I didn't. Are you asking for everything?

*Samuel Neill--undated*

*(died 1912 West Point, Hancock County, Illinois)*

# Websites

*Only those mentioned in the text are included.*

## Archive.org

www.archive.org

> Digital images of a variety of print and other media. Full text search available.

## Bureau of Land Management

www.glorecords.blm.gov

> Digital images of Federal land patents and other materials related to Federal land records.

## Blogger

www.blogger.com

> A host for creating your own personal blog.

## [Census] Enumeration Forms

usa.ipums.org/usa/voliii/tEnumForm.shtml

> Copies of US Census enumeration forms for 1860-2010

## FamilySearch

www.familysearch.org

> The website of the Family History Library provided by The Church of Jesus Christ of Latter-day Saints.

## Google

www.google.com

> Internet search engine—not the only one.

## GoogleBooks

books.google.com

> A section of Google's search that focuses on digitized print materials.

## Sanborn Fire Insurance Maps at the Library of Congress

www.loc.gov/collections/sanborn-maps

> A bibliography of fire insurance maps from this company.

## Selective Service Records at National Archives

www.archives.gov/st-louis/selective-service

> Information on obtaining United States Selective Service records.

## WordPress

www.wordpress.com

> A host for creating your own blog.

## WorldCat

www.worldcat.org

> An online worldwide library card catalog.

# Index

**Michael John Neill** began researching his family genealogy in the early 1980s and grew up a few miles from the county courthouse in the county where many of his family members have lived since the 1860s. He has spent many days rummaging through old original records in a variety of locations across the United States attempting to discover more ancestral details other than vital event dates. Foraging those records for clues has taught him a great deal about research, his ancestors, and himself.

Michael writes and lectures on a variety of genealogical topics, with particular interest in immigration, women's rights, research methodology, and problem-solving. He has also led annual research trips to the Family History Library in Salt Lake City, Utah, and the Allen County Public Library in Ft. Wayne, Indiana, since the late 1990s. His lectures and trips emphasize helping researchers improve their research skills so they can more effectively conduct their own research because he knows that no one cares as much about a genealogist's family as the genealogist themselves.

Michael has a master's degree in mathematics and has been a community college instructor since the early 1990s.

Michael maintains a web presence at www.genealogytipoftheday.com

Made in the USA
Monee, IL
16 December 2020

53942943R00166